Titus,

God Bless and
Keep accelerating your
mind!

Mike

Michael J. Mattia

HEAVEN 3.0
Seeing and Believing

Michael L. Mathews

authorHOUSE®

AuthorHouse™
1663 Liberty Drive
Bloomington, IN 47403
www.authorhouse.com
Phone: 1-800-839-8640

Published by AuthorHouse 9/4/2012

ISBN: 978-1-4772-6059-3 (hc)
ISBN: 978-1-4772-6060-9 (sc)
ISBN: 978-1-4772-6061-6 (e)

Library of Congress Control Number: 2012914956

Unless otherwise noted, All Scripture verses are from the
New International Version (NIV) *translation.*

Contents

Dedication and Special Thanks 1

Foreword 3

Preface. 7

Introduction: The Reflections of Heaven as Time and
Knowledge Advance 11

Unit 1: Heaven 3.0 Entrance 23

    Chapter 1. The Tribal Effect: Angel See Angel Do! 31

    Chapter 2. The Door Has Been Opened; Why Not
    Take a Peek?. 43

    Chapter 3. Coming out of the Closet: The Facts are on
    God's Side 57

    Chapter 4. When My Story Reflects His Story. 73

    Chapter 5. Water and Blood Have Life, Memory, and
    Reflection 85

    Chapter 6. Light versus Love 101

Unit 2: The Principles and Keys to Seeing Heaven 3.0 117

    Chapter 7. The Law of Refraction and Reflection. 119

    Chapter 8. The Principle of Illusion of Knowledge and
    Time 125

    Chapter 9. The Law of Reference-Point Living: The
    OODA Loop 135

Chapter 10. The Principle of the Enigma Experience . . . 149

Chapter 11. The Principle of the Merchant and Pearl . . . 157

Chapter 12. The Principle of Thanksgiving Worship. . . . 167

Chapter 13. The Principle of Clouds: Keeping Your
Head in the Clouds. 181

Chapter 14. Fearfully and Wonderfully Made 191

Bibliography 201

DEDICATION AND SPECIAL THANKS

First, I would like to thank God for the patience He has shown during the past twenty years by developing my life in a fuller manner. At first it appeared to be an awkward method, but after twenty years, He has proven that not only is He faithful, but He is also a masterful builder who molds a person individually and in a very thoughtful pattern to produce something a person could never do by himself or herself.

> "But Christ is faithful as a son over God's house. And we are His house, if we hold on to our courage and hope of which we boast." (Hebrews 3:6)

Second, this book would not have been possible without the cooperation in ministry of my beautiful wife and partner, Pam. She has been a true encourager and partner in God's work. She has filled a place in my heart and life that no other person could have filled. Together, God has allowed us to produce this book and many other miraculous endeavors that have exceeded our greatest expectations. All my work with other ministers and coworkers combined cannot compare to the teamwork we have built together. God has built this house that we share in our hearts!

Third, without the life and joy of my two daughters, Jessica and Tiffany, this author and father would have never seen the beauty of life and dreams that made the beginning of any endeavor possible. Thank you, Jessica and Tiffany!

A special thanks to Tiffany L. Mathews and Pastor Simeon Strauser. Tiffany assisted tirelessly on research and pre-editing services, while Pastor Simeon Strauser provided the thought-provoking foreword as well as years of calm and patient instruction.

FOREWORD

By Pastor Simeon Strauser

Thou wilt keep him in perfect peace, whose mind is stayed on thee: because he trusteth in thee. —Isaiah 26:3 (KJV)

As pastor, educator, missionary, and chairman of the church fellowship of Full Gospel Assemblies, I have heard and preached many sermons relative to heaven. It is the desire of my heart to see the heavens open up and rain down salvation and righteousness as described in Isaiah 45:8. The metaphoric approach that Michael Mathews uses to illustrate heaven reinforces the sense that the people of God are called to keep their minds upon the Lord. As we seek the salvation and the righteousness of the Lord, we should be expecting with confidence to witness a showering of His promised touch from the heavens.

My parents, the late Dr. Charles and AnnaMae Strauser, were the founders and visionaries of the Maranatha Full Gospel Bible Institute and Full Gospel Assemblies fellowship birthed as the Full Gospel Church some sixty-five years ago. Giving witness of the daily miracle touch of God both in their personal lives and ministry, they tirelessly dedicated their lives to the service of the Lord. Their proclaiming of the prophetic Word of God through pastoral, educational, and evangelistic ministries fostered the development of the work of the Lord the world over. Being present with the Lord now for many years, I believe that they along with all the saints of God are serving as earth's cloud of witnesses—and challenging us who remain to rise up and to look up in expectation for the blessings of God to be poured out from the open windows of heaven.

This exciting and intriguing thought is the very essence of what Michael is conveying in this insightful book, *Heaven 3.0*.

Serving with the ministry leadership of the Maranatha FG Bible Institute, Full Gospel Assemblies, and Christ Chapel FG Assembly, I am forward looking, standing on the promises of God, as we celebrate our sixty-five years of ministry over 2012–13. We are believing that we will see the Holy Spirit rain down from heaven over this celebration season and into the years ahead. It gives me great hope to realize that collectively all the cumulative prayer, fasting, labor, giving, sorrows, tears, and joys from the past sixty-five years have been the building blocks bringing forth the promises unto God's people from both a heavenly and earthly perspective. The harvest will be beyond our understanding, and greater than our eyes have envisioned. In the times ahead, I am believing Full Gospel ministries and God's people throughout the earth will witness a taste of the heavenly promise of God, "Eye hath not seen , nor ear heard , neither have entered into the heart of man, the things which God hath prepared for them that love him" (1 Corinthians 2:9).

I first met Michael Mathews in June of 1996 as he received his ministerial license with Full Gospel Assemblies. As a young minister in the Fellowship, we could see the potential and desire of Mike to bring concepts, people, and even fellowships together to see greater things. Since 1996, I have witnessed the passion of Mike to develop advanced technology for distance-learning student studies, enabling training in the Word of God to be available to millions throughout the world via the Internet. Mike's ministry of teaching, preaching, and writing has demonstrated a desire to realize mighty breakthroughs in the work of the Lord. With Mike's writing of *Heaven 3.0*, I see yet another breakthrough for this season of time. This breakthrough is one abounding with heavenly declarations for the child of God.

Through God's favor and fortitude, Mike has touched many over the years. However, in this new endeavor of articulating scriptural insights of heaven, Mike reaches readers with a challenge to open their hearts and minds for a fresh and intriguing understanding of the blessings of God, which include the opening of the heavens upon earth. This understanding brings to the forefront of thought the teaching of our Lord and Savior,

Christ Jesus as he taught "This, then, is how you should pray: Our Father in heaven, hallowed be your name, your kingdom come, your will be done on earth as it is in heaven" (Matthew 6:9–10).

I encourage all clergy, all children of God, to see yourself in the image of the Lord God empowered and "saved by the mercy of God, by the washing of regeneration, and the renewing of the Holy Ghost" (Titus 3:5). My prayer is to witness a fresh view of heaven and to see the people of God join forces today to reflect the beauty of heaven in confident expectation for the outpouring of the power of God upon all mankind throughout the earth.

Blessings be upon you,
Pastor Simeon Strauser

Simeon Strauser is married to Marissa Francisco-Strauser, and together they serve Christ Chapel Full Gospel Assembly, Parkesburg, PA, lead congregation to the church fellowship of Full Gospel Assemblies. He is a graduate of the Maranatha Full Gospel Bible Institute. Pastor Simeon also serves as Chairman of Full Gospel Assemblies, President of Maranatha Full Gospel Bible Institute, and International Bishop with the Philippine Alliance of Full Gospel Churches, and he is the founder of the Little Jewels Christian Preschool. He is a national and international speaker, teacher, and missionary with a passion for education to the indigenous peoples of the African and Asian nations.

PREFACE

So that your days and the days of your children may be many in the land that the LORD swore to give your forefathers, as many as the days that the heavens are above the earth.

—Isaiah 45:8

Although my near death experience was nearly thirty four years ago, there is virtually not a day that goes by that I am not aware of making decisions based on that experience.

—Geraldine Berkheimer

Welcome to Heaven 3.0! I trust I grabbed your attention by using one of the most pleasant names and places known to all humanity. I can't go wrong writing about one of the most pleasant yet mysterious places known throughout the world. I could cross all continents, religions, tribes, and tongues and find that most people have a common ground by using the words "heaven" or "paradise" or "the hereafter." Even though heaven would conjure up many images, we would still find that there is commonality around the thoughts and images of a peaceful destiny called heaven. Everyone loves the great deathbed stories of friends or relatives that share about their glimpses into heaven just prior to passing away. The mere thoughts of eternal peace and rest give people hope, comfort, and joy.

One of the reasons we find common ground on the topic of heaven is that most people have a pleasant and futuristic view of heaven. As an old saying goes, "I can't wait until I go to heaven; I just don't want to be the first one to get there!" The reason our thoughts remain consistently pleasant is because very few people have tarnished the "virtual" or "futuristic" place we view as heaven, which remains a mystery for many people, but a very positive and hopeful mystery. Our view of heaven is quite the opposite of many of the other faith-on-earth elements, including religions, churches, denominations, beliefs, clergy, etc. We have built many idols, false illusions, scams, earthly heroes, palaces, churches, shrines, temples, buildings, and organizations, and we have even taken political stands over most of the faith-on-earth elements of religion. Stepping further into the reality of our day we have even taken the one person who came from heaven, Jesus Christ, and made Him a stumbling block among most of humanity. As humans who have touched most of the elements of religion or faith-on-earth, we can easily develop tainted views of faith-on-earth. Simply put, faith-on-earth has been modified by so many human filters that we have become rightful skeptics who find it hard to distinguish the purest form of the truth. This has resulted in hundreds of religions and sects and is the main reason there are still eight "rival" religious groups in the world that have a religious war mindset. These groups will be described in a later chapter, but for now let's focus on the common ground called heaven.

The fact that the idea of heaven has remained untarnished should be considered a mystery in and of itself. Considering that most religions want to own, claim, stake, and/or brag about their knowledge and wisdom in areas of faith, it is amazing that we have not tarnished the common image of heaven. The few people who have made false claims about when the world is coming to an end have come the closest to tarnishing its image, but even these claims have not tarnished the majority of people's views of heaven. Heaven is the one place that still provides humanity with images of hope, peace, surrealistic visions, grandeur, peace, and the ultimate meeting place with our image of God as well as loved ones we have lost on earth.

I have purposely taken the common view of heaven and attached the 3.0 suffix. I believe you will enjoy the journey and be challenged to realize that we live in a day in which knowledge and revelation are at an all-time high. The prophet Daniel speaks of a day when knowledge would increase, while the apostle John shares that the mystery of the Gospel would be fulfilled as spoken by prophets such as Daniel. (Daniel 12:4; Revelation 10:10). As we are approaching these events, there is no doubt that knowledge will continue to increase. In addition, the mysteries of the world will continue to unfold and have clearer meaning.

I stand amazed at the amount of attention people place on the fear of a "one world" government, the anti-Christ, and end-time happenings while seldom giving thought to the promise of God's kingdom. End-time events may be true and plausible, but they should never overshadow God's promise of His kingdom of heaven or stop people from praying that His will be done on earth as it is in heaven. Doing so only gives more credit and mind power to the negative side of life and robs people of living in the strength, faith, and power of God's promises for the very people He created in His image.

It is the intent of *Heaven 3.0* to allow people to see and explore faith on earth in a purer form by understanding that faith in heaven is becoming nearer to us and therefore easier to see. The untarnished view of heaven with increasing knowledge is already starting to allow millions of people to see and experience heavenly aspects of God's kingdom in a clearer manner. The purity of heaven along with increased knowledge is giving us a clearer filter of who we really are in God's kingdom. In the process of seeing who we really are, we start to see who God ultimately made us to become.

The context of *Heaven 3.0* can best be explained by visualizing a reference point of what would be considered Heaven 1.0 and Heaven 2.0, which will be described in the introduction chapter.

But you, Daniel, close up and seal the words of the scroll until the time of the end. Many will go here and there to increase knowledge. (Daniel 12:4)

And he swore by him who lives for ever and ever, who created the heavens and all that is in them, the earth and all that is in it, and the sea and all that is in it, and said, "There will be no more delay! But in the days when the seventh angel is about to sound his trumpet, the mystery of God will be accomplished, just as he announced to his servants the prophets. (Revelation 10:6–7)

THE REFLECTIONS OF HEAVEN AS TIME AND KNOWLEDGE ADVANCE

I know a man in Christ who fourteen years ago was caught up to the third heaven. Whether it was in the body or out of the body I do not know—God knows. And I know that this man—whether in the body or apart from the body I do not know, but God knows—was caught up to paradise. He heard inexpressible things, things that man is not permitted to tell. I will boast about a man like that, but I will not boast about myself, except about my weaknesses.

—2 Corinthians 12:2–5

The Changes in Time

The definition of heaven is fairly broad but simple. Both the *Biblical Dictionary* and *Webster's Dictionary* description of heaven is below. The definitions are broad and simple, and this allows our imagination to pick up quite a vast array of images.

Biblical Dictionary Definition:

Primarily the region of the air and clouds, and of the planets and stars, but chiefly the world of holy bliss above the visible heavens. It is called "the third heaven," "the highest heaven," and "the heaven of heavens," expressions nearly synonymous. There holy beings are to dwell, seeing all of God that it is possible for creatures to see. Thither Christ ascended, to intercede for his people and prepare for them a place where all shall at length be gathered, to go no more out forever, Ephesians 4:10, Hebrews 8:1 9:24–28.

(The words "heaven" and "heavens" are used approximately 716 times in scripture according to the American Tract Society).

Webster's Dictionary Definition:

1. The abode of God, the angels, and the spirits of the righteous after death; the place or state of existence of the blessed after the mortal life.

2. Usually, heavens. The sky, firmament, or expanse of space surrounding the earth.

Please close your eyes for approximately ten seconds and see what images or thoughts your mind conjectures about heaven. They may include images of Jesus, streets of gold, mansions, being reunited with deceased loved ones, angels, streams of living water, God, harps, musical instruments, worship, pearly gates, saints of old, etc. The images you had while closing your eyes were more than likely based on your understanding of heaven from the Bible, Sunday school, or movies. These images would be your first generation of knowledge concerning heaven. For the sake of establishing a reference point we will call this Heaven 1.0, as it is generally the first generation of heaven that most people have learned.

Imagine in your mind that you are one of the many millions of people who in addition to their first generation of knowledge concerning heaven have had either a personal visitation to or from heaven or read about others visitations from heaven such as the *New York Times* best-seller *Heaven is for Real*, in which an eight-year-old boy shares his experience of visiting heaven. These new images of heaven would be a second generation of knowledge concerning heaven, or Heaven 2.0.

By the year 2011 it is estimated that over 13 million people have had some sort of out-of-body experience that has caused them to have new and enhanced images of heaven. The Gallup Organization and near-death research studies have estimated that there have been some 13 million adult near-death experiences in the U.S. If you add children's near-death experiences and all experiences worldwide, the figure would be much larger. The Near Death Experience Research Foundation reports that approximately 770 people every day experience some form of out-of-body experience.

This fresher view of heaven or even portions of heaven are adding to our increased knowledge of God's glory and heaven itself. This is the very essence of Daniel 12:4: "But you, Daniel, close up and seal the words of the scroll until the time of the end. Many will go here and there to increase knowledge." We are living at a time when the knowledge of heaven is increasing as evidenced by the number of stories being told of visitations to heaven, including:

+ *90 Minutes in Heaven: My True Story* by Don Piper
+ *Heaven is for Real: A Little Boy's Astounding Story of His Trip to Heaven and Back* by Todd Burpo and Lynn Vincent
+ *The Boy Who Came Back from Heaven: A Remarkable Account of Miracles, Angels, and Life beyond This World* by Kevin Malarkey and Alex Malarkey
+ *Heaven is For Real* by Phil Rehberg
+ *Nine Days in Heaven: The Vision of Marietta Davis* by Dennis Prince

+ *Angels in the ER: Inspiring True Stories from an Emergency Room Doctor* by Robert D. Lesslie
+ *My Time in Heaven* by Richard Sigmund

There is a clear upward path between Heaven 1.0 and Heaven 2.0 that gives us a glimpse of an ongoing and increasing knowledge of heaven. As time and knowledge continue to advance, the ongoing increase in revelation and knowledge will bring further truth of heaven and God's mysteries into a clear and reflective focus.

The increased awareness and focus is the reason for writing *Heaven 3.0*. Figure 1 charts the trajectory starting with Heaven 1.0 through Heaven 3.0 that represents the reality that as time and knowledge advance, humanity will continue to see more of the reality of heaven. For a purposeful reference point we will call this new reality Heaven 3.0 and use the scripture that states that God's glory will fill the earth as much as the water covers the sea (Habakkuk 2:14). This advancement in knowledge and time as well as revelation will be fairly spectacular and warrants an investigation into how heaven and earth may meet up with one another. The purpose of this book is to help people improve their ability to spiritually see the fullest view of God, the kingdom of God, and heaven to better prepare for the spiritual glimpses that are already appearing and the fuller glimpses and experiences yet to come.

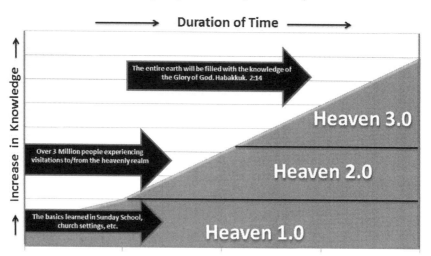

Figure 1 View of Heaven as Time and Knowledge Advance

Table 1 represents the contextual ideas of the three generations of heaven that may be seen, heard, or experienced as time and knowledge advance.

Definition	Identifiers to Definition
Heaven 1.0	This is the logical viewpoint based on what you have read or heard, including possible imagery of the learned words that help you visualize what heaven could be like. 1. What you heard in Sunday school class. 2. What you read in the fictional *Left Behind* series. 3. What you were taught by your parents. etc.
Heaven 2.0	Recent and increased knowledge and experiences based on people who have experienced "pieces" of heaven in visions, dreams, or out-of-body experiences. 1. Books such as *Heaven is for Real*. 2. People who have died, went to heaven, and came back to life. 3. The over 13,000,000 people who have now claimed to have had out-of-body experiences in some form in which they have seen glimpses of heaven.

Definition	Identifiers to Definition
Heaven 3.0	The "real deal" reality of how heaven meets earth, replaces earth, or is a separate place that manifests God's promises. 1. The whole earth will be filled with the knowledge of the glory of God. (Habakkuk 2:14) 2. There will be no more tears, sorrow, nor death. (Revelation 21.4) 3. There will be signs in the heavens above (Acts 2:17–19)

Table 1: The Three Generations of Heaven

The scripture passages in Table 2 will help you want to seek out the further spiritual glimpses that God intended as time and knowledge advances.

Verses	Scripture	Paraphrase— Meaning
Acts 2:17–19	In the last days I will pour my Spirit out upon all flesh and your sons and daughters will prophecy, your old men will dream dreams, and your young men will have visions. And there will be signs and wonders in the heavens above.	People will start seeing glimpses of heaven through dreams, visions, and prophecies, and there will actually be signs in the heavens.

Verses	Scripture	Paraphrase—Meaning
Eph. 1:19	The eyes of your understanding being enlightened; that you may know the hope of His calling, and what the riches of Glory of His inheritance in the saints.	God's desire is to have our spiritual eyes open and enlightened so we can see the inheritance of both the present and future.
I Cor. 2:9–10	Eye hath not seen, nor ear heard, neither entered into the heart of man the great things that God has prepared for them that love Him. But God has revealed them unto by His Spirit for the Spirit searches the deep things of God.	Evidence that our natural man cannot see the spiritual things that come through spiritual revelation. They are also too wonderful for human eyes and heart to process.
Hab. 2:14	The entire earth will be filled with the knowledge of the Glory of God—as much as the water covers the sea.	Shows a point where God's glory, presence, and/or kingdom completely fills the earth.
Rom. 8:14–23	The entire creation groans and waits for the manifestation of the sons of God to be revealed through the Glory of God's saints.	Shows God's presence, glory, or kingdom will be manifested in His people and will be released when the groaning forces the people to manifest His power.

Verses	Scripture	Paraphrase—Meaning
1 Thes. 4:17; 5:2	He will come like a thief in the night, and we will meet Him in the clouds.	Indicates Jesus will return and we will meet Him. Many assume we are going somewhere, but what if the clouds of heaven come to earth, and then we meet Him face to face?
Dan. 12:4	But you, Daniel, close up and seal the words of the scroll until the time of the end. Many will go here and there to increase knowledge.	Daniel was informed that there would be an increase in travel and knowledge.
Col. 1:12	Giving thanks unto the Father which hath made us meet to be partakers of the inheritance of the saints in light; Who has delivered us from the power of darkness, and has transformed us into the kingdom of His Son.	God has transformed us into the likeness of His Son and has given us the inheritance of light in order to see His fullness.

Table 2: Scripture Passages about Heaven

These quotations from both the Bible and real-life examples give us a small glimpse into the reality that as time progresses there will be a continual increase in knowledge, visions, dreams, signs, and wonders in the heavens and in our understanding of God.

My Personal Whisper from God

In 2009 I was praying and meditating on the things of God. During this time it was bothersome to me that people could believe in the marvels of technology, wireless and satellite communications into thin air, vampires, perceived sexual freedom, chemical enhancements for every perceived illness, and vaccines to help addictive behaviors. It seemed that the world was mesmerized by all the tricks, treats, illusions, pharmaceuticals, beauty, sexual naivety, greed, and blood indulgence that humanity could dream of. Within a few seconds I heard one of the most pleasant and precious whispers I have ever heard. The still, small voice of God was whispering to me that it was time to tell people that the world has nothing up on God. It was a whisper with a vision, showing me that the marvels of technology, vampire fallacies, and other sorcery-related illusions had nothing on God's supernatural ability to transform and shift and to transcend time, people, and space. He was reassuring me that there would soon be heavenly supernatural manifestations that would put the best human-created illusions to shame. However, it was also a reminder that those who indulged, believed, and worshiped these shameful practices such as media hype, chemicals, etc., may never get to spiritually see and receive the real deal that comes as God's glory begins to move and show forth the power of heaven on the earth. This will be the revelation that I am calling Heaven 3.0, a clean, pure, worshipful experience that God's glory is second place to nobody!

Time to Give God the Glory

During the past fifty years there have been shifts of knowledge and understanding in almost every facet of life. Imagine fifty years ago walking down the road with a four-inch by three-inch phone that could connect you to any part of the world, retrieve more data than the first ten supercomputers combined, play music, access videos on something called YouTube, and send text messages all at the same time. Oh, and I forgot to mention this device, this transmitter of knowledge, did not need to be plugged in anywhere as all this information would pass through air and water waves (yes, thin air). Fifty years ago it would have been hard to fathom this type of transmitter of knowledge. This capability has been brought to us through multiple transmitter/receiver technology generations called 2G, 3G, and now 4G.

Who could have imagined that technology and human video, voice, sound, and information could be displayed in every square inch of every square mile around the world? Wherever I am with my receiver, I can expect the large satellites freely floating in space will miraculously connect me to any other square inch of every square mile across the globe.

I now live in a world where I expect and have complete confidence that transparent signals can travel in front of me any time of day or night as they miraculously enter my mobile device. I must admit and realize that the transparent nature of air and water waves have not changed; rather, the technological advances of each new generation of mobile devices have refined and advanced the amount of knowledge and information in my new space in time.

Even though we can appreciate and believe that our mobile devices have advanced to expect information and knowledge to float through space, our spiritual receivers cannot yet believe that the invisible aspects of God, His kingdom, and His angels can be just as readily available. The reason we have a hard time is that we have not allowed an increase in the generations of knowledge to increase in the spiritual realm as we have in the technical realm. Our spiritual receptors of God's transmission are in a time warp even though God stated they should increase. Many people have stayed in their first generation of spiritual receptivity and are not fine-tuned enough to receive the increase in spiritual wisdom or knowledge.

I trust this last paragraph may open your eyes, ears, and heart a little bit to appreciate the reality that we as humans have advanced our faith in the advanced generations of technology, pharmaceuticals, sexuality, politics, and social causes while still living in the first generation of spiritual knowledge. I believe it is time to give God all the honor and glory due His name and start seeing that God is not stale in comparison to the world. Rather, we have chosen to give credit and glory to other advancements before we have given God credit and glory. God's method of transmitting through the air and water waves is no different today than it was in the beginning of time. What was supposed to have changed was our ability to tune in our receivers and transmitters to the reality that God is Lord of all things both visible and invisible.

As God's power, glory, and dominion have become more visible and powerful, we should have been tuning our ears to hear what He has been speaking to the church and opening our spiritual eyes to see the fuller picture of our full inheritance. Remember, the world's advancements have nothing up on God's advancements. His glory has been expanding and descending upon the earth for some time. This is the very reason why so many things on earth are being exposed, including corporate corruption, sexual infidelity, sexual misconduct among clergy, the housing market crash, pharmaceutical overdosing, political mayhem, and many other things that we have put our trust in. God's glory has no choice but to "heal" and "deal" with humanity. When God's glory is received by our transmitters, it carries healing and deliverance with it. When God's glory is not received by our transmitters, our actions are easily exposed for what they are.

The glory of God will continue to descend with increased measure until we see the fullness of heaven completely poured out. This process will continue until both the healing side and the dealing side all bow down and confess that Jesus Christ is Lord. This will be the fullness or last generation of knowledge in time in the history of the world.

One thing is for sure—the manifestation of God's glory will not look like Heaven 1.0. Rather, it will look more like Heaven 3.0 or even a more-advanced generation of knowledge.

> Jesus … who is the invisible image of God, the first born of every creature: For by Him were all things created, that are in heaven and in earth, visible and invisible, whether they be thrones, or dominions, or principalities or powers: all things were created for Him and by Him. He is before all things and in Him all things consist. (Colossians 1:15–16)

This book, *Heaven 3.0*, deals with the realities of seeing the fullness of the kingdom of God through the reflection created in the culmination of heaven and earth! God has advanced the timeline of knowledge for all of us to see, believe, and receive greater glimpses of heaven. All we have to do is tune in our receivers to the most recent generation of knowledge.

UNIT 1

HEAVEN 3.0 ENTRANCE

You heavens above, rain down righteousness; let the clouds shower it down. Let the earth open wide, let salvation spring up, let righteousness grow with it; I, the LORD, have created it.

—Isaiah 45:8

Heaven is the neutral realm of possibility that brings tranquility and promise to anyone who believes in some form of eternal life, regardless of their religion.

—Michael L. Mathews

Before we can enter a new realm of understanding, we must recognize that there is an open door into that realm of understanding. Chapters 1–6 will peak your curiosity and interest to see into deeper and greater realms of God's promises and visitations from heaven. We are not merely physical beings trying to grasp the spiritual and heavenly realm; rather, we are spiritual and heavenly beings passing through the physical realm. And this is all factual, because we were created in the image of a spiritual and heavenly God. Your responsibility will be to see and believe what God has for you!

A good way to view the reality of heaven and why God has made sure it is untarnished is to keep in mind the fact that He promises to bring only one true church into heaven. This means somehow God will facilitate a shift toward a "oneness" so He has only one "church" without spot or wrinkle. This will happen when we are all closest to heaven. The reason, though simple, explains why so many people are starting to have glimpses into heaven.

To explain, consider the fact that there are eight major (rival) religions that exist that make up approximately 72 to 77 percent of the world's population, which is estimated at 6.9 billion people. This means that there is between 4.9 and 5.3 billion people believing in eight major religions.

What makes the religions unique as well as competitive is how they view the pathway to eternity, heaven, or the life hereafter. On the other hand, the one thing they have in common is that they all believe that the end result of their pathway is a form of heaven. This means that the closer we get to heaven, the greater the chance we have of becoming uninfluenced by our beliefs and can see God for who He always was, is, and will be.

Figure 2 illustrates the pathway for all eight major religions and the ultimate destiny called heaven. You will notice the pathway for all eight major religions consistently follow the following three elements.

1. **Perceived Problem for Humanity:** Each religion has a belief of what the major worldly problem is that all humanity faces. As an example, for Christianity the main problem is sin, while for Islam the main problem is pride or self-sufficiency.

2. **Perceived Leader or Supreme Authority:** With each religion having a perception of what the main human problem is, each religion has a perception of the supreme authority or process that will assist it with the human problem. This may be a god, a prophet, a messenger, multiple gods, or multiple processes. An example is sin being the main problem for Christians; their God provided a sacrifice for man's sin, Jesus. With pride being the main sin for Islam, Muslims have one God, Allah, who must be completely surrendered too.

3. **Technique for Ridding Oneself of Problems and Gaining Access to Heaven:** Each religion with a supreme being who assists in the perceived main human problems has a technique to solve the problem in order to gain acceptance to heaven, paradise, or an eternal, better afterlife.

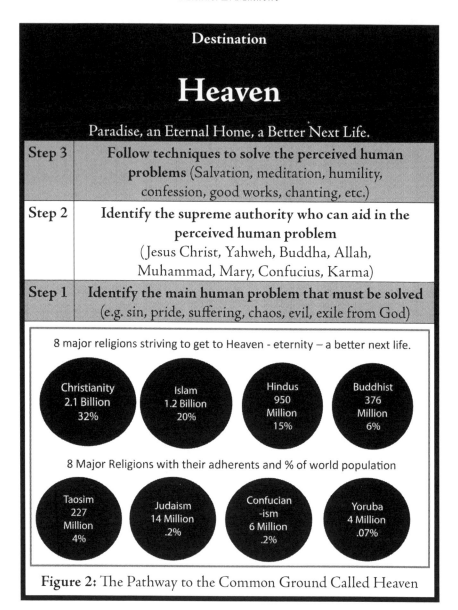

Destination

Heaven

Paradise, an Eternal Home, a Better Next Life.

Step 3	Follow techniques to solve the perceived human problems (Salvation, meditation, humility, confession, good works, chanting, etc.)
Step 2	Identify the supreme authority who can aid in the perceived human problem (Jesus Christ, Yahweh, Buddha, Allah, Muhammad, Mary, Confucius, Karma)
Step 1	Identify the main human problem that must be solved (e.g. sin, pride, suffering, chaos, evil, exile from God)

8 major religions striving to get to Heaven - eternity – a better next life.

Christianity 2.1 Billion 32%

Islam 1.2 Billion 20%

Hindus 950 Million 15%

Buddhist 376 Million 6%

8 Major Religions with their adherents and % of world population

Taosim 227 Million 4%

Judaism 14 Million .2%

Confucian-ism 6 Million .2%

Yoruba 4 Million .07%

Figure 2: The Pathway to the Common Ground Called Heaven

It is my desire to have this figure help all readers see that there is a reason we are told to set our affections on heaven, as it is the place we all stand the best chance to let our religious perceptions and techniques become less important than the fact of the Supreme Authority of heaven versus the doctrines, techniques, and beliefs that hinder and alienate. "Since, then, you have been raised with Christ, set your hearts on things above, where Christ is seated at the right hand of God. Set your minds on things above, not on earthly things" (Colossians 3:1–2).

Table 3 on the next page provides more information about the eight major religions and the reality that the closest common ground we all have is heaven. The data is derived from numerous sources that try to depict the most accurate representations available about the eight religions. Other religions could be noted, but not enough information on the smaller religions is readily available. A good source for more information on the eight major religions is *God is Not One: The Eight Rival Religions That Run the World*, by Stephen Prothero, HarperOne, 2011.

Unit 1 contains the following chapters

Chapter 1: The Tribal Effect: Angel See Angel Do!

Chapter 2: The Door Has Been Opened; Why Not Take a Peek?

Chapter 3: Coming out of the Closet: The Facts Are on God's Side

Chapter 4: When My Story Reflects His Story

Chapter 5: Water and Blood Have Life, Memory, and Reflection

Chapter 6: Light versus Love

Name of religion	Followers and percent of world population	Problem with humanity	Solution to problem	Prime leader(s)	Technique for solving	Common outcome and desire
1. Christianity Includes Protestants, Catholics, Evangelicals, and Pentecostals	2.1 billion 32 percent	Sin	Primarily salvation thru Jesus. (Some variants of the four religious groups look too good works for salvation.)	Primarily God the Father, Son, and Holy Spirit. (Some variants of the four groups look to Mary, the pope, and the saints.)	Repentance of personal sin, and confession of Christ's sacrificial death for forgiveness of personal sin. Some include living by faith, works, and grace.	Heaven
2. Islam	1 billion, 20–22 percent	Pride, self-sufficiency	Submission to the one true God, Allah	Allah—God, Muhammad as a messenger	Submission to God through prayer	Heaven or Paradise
3. Hinduism	950 million 15 percent	Suffering and evil	Good deeds and reincarnate to a better life	Many gods can be worshipped	Buildup of good deeds (good karma)	Heaven or paradise
4. Buddhism	376 million 6 percent	Suffering	Nirvana or removal from suffering	Buddha as the first to find nirvana	Meditation and chanting	Nirvana in the next life
5. Daosim, Taosim	227 million 4 percent	Chaos	Finding harmony and flourishing	Serve a process, "The way"	Good deeds and living in harmony	Nirvana
6. Judaism	14 million .2 percent	Exile from God	Return to God	One True God (YHVH)	Repentance, study, follow God's commands	Heaven
7. Confucianism	6 million .1 percent	Chaos	Social order, harmony	No God—Only Heaven	Harmonious living	Paradise, next life
8. Yoruba	4 million .07 percent	None	Connection with the next life	Over 400 gods	None	Next life

Table 3: Eight Religions Working toward an Outcome of Heaven

(Sources: The World Religious Database; The World Christian Database, One; religioustolerance.org; *God is Not One: The Eight Rival Religions That Run the World* by Stephen Prothero, HarperOne, 2011.)

CHAPTER 1

THE TRIBAL EFFECT: ANGEL SEE ANGEL DO!

Since, then, you have been raised with Christ, set your hearts on things above, where Christ is seated at the right hand of God. Set your minds on things above, not on earthly things.

—Colossians 3:1–2

The one who follows the crowd will get no further than the crowd. The one who walks alone is likely to find himself in places no one has ever seen.

—Albert Einstein

In 2006 I was taking a flight from Dallas to Minneapolis via Chicago. I was coming off a bad month of travel experiences and sensed this was about to be one more bad experience. About thirty minutes before the flight was to land in Chicago, I started talking to a passenger next to me, who was from Bulgaria. He was staring at my nice leather Bible I was using to prepare a sermon. As we approached Chicago I asked him if he had a Bible; he said no and appeared to be admiring my Bible again.

As soon as the plane started moving down the runway, it diverted to a side area of the airport and sat there for a few minutes before the pilot spoke: "This is your captain. I know we are running late, but we were informed by air traffic control to divert to a holding area on the runway while they get our gate ready."

A million thoughts ran through my mind as I looked at my watch and knew I had only twenty minutes to catch my flight to Minneapolis. At that very moment I sensed God say, *Give the Bulgarian passenger your Bible!* I was hesitant at first, but I asked the Bulgarian, "How would you like my Bible, seeing you don't have one?" He said, "Oh, I couldn't take such a nice Bible; it is so nice, big, and pure leather." I insisted he take it, so he eagerly took it and started fondling the leather covers and started fanning through the pages. As soon as I saw the glow on his face, the airplane started moving toward our gate, and I sensed a great sign of relief and pleasure that my nicest Bible was in the hands of a Bulgarian traveler.

Well, my excitement stopped after the plane made it about 400 yards and came to a stop. The pilot expressed again his regrets about being late. He said it was a false alarm and we had still not been cleared to proceed to the gate. At that very instant I heard a clear whisper in my spirit saying, *this plane will not budge unless you share the Gospel with the Bulgarian passenger.* I took a second to make sure it was God speaking as the sweat ran down my forehead. I quickly looked at the passenger and said "Let's look at John 3:16 in your new Bible." Within three minutes I had shared the Gospel, and he smiled as if he knew exactly what was happening from the very beginning. As soon as he received the Gospel message, the plane immediately raced to the gate, and I made my flight.

As I sat on my next flight I heard the whisper again. This time it was a gentle reminder that God is in charge of all my travels, and if I spend every flight and travel experience worrying about my own personal details, I will miss the blessings and responsibilities of my spiritual walk and life.

For the next six years of travel I started focusing on divine connections within the spiritual realms of life and spent less time on my travel experiences and disappointments. This experience taught me I was far too focused on earthly things and not the heavenly things, where divine connections occur. Through those years many of my colleagues would worry and say, "Mike, how come you don't remember which hotels you are at until you're getting off the flight, and why do you never know the details of your return flight?" I would simply smile and reply that I had bigger concerns than dwelling on all the physical details of my travel. Through those years my wife and kids would wonder how I made it around, but they always appreciated the stories of divine appointments.

In essence, I knew my responsibility of being a messenger as well as being ministered to by messengers was where I wanted to spend my energies during my times of travel. Many times I would sit back and laugh and rejoice as I knew I had entered a new realm of understanding and was part of God's heavenly host or heavenly tribe of travelers. It's not easy, but I would rather mimic and follow the behaviors of heavenly hosts than mimic and follow the behavior of earthly worriers.

Many of us have heard the saying "monkey see monkey do." Why is it easier for people to come down to the level of animals versus stepping up to the level of angels? Why don't we say "angel see angel do"? Before we can answer this question we need a little background information on our human desire to be part of things we can see and touch versus those we can only imagine or read about. This understanding will also help prove the point that it is always easier to see the lowest rather than the highest common denominator from a physical and spiritual perspective.

The saying "monkey see monkey do" originated in Jamaica in the early eighteenth century and popped up in American culture in the early 1920s. The saying refers to learning a process without understanding why it works. People are prone to repeat what they see or believe within their groups, including groups of athletes, coworkers, family, churches, community organizations, hobbyists, schoolmates, and so on.

A more comprehensive concept of this reality is referred to as tribal behavior or the tribal effect. The tribal effect indicates that as humans we like to be part of groups or tribes we can feel a part of, join, and then compare ourselves to and compete against. People yearn to be part of elite groups such as the U.S. Army Rangers, the Navy Seals, or "the few the proud" Marines or attend elite colleges, be on leading committees in a company, join a fraternity or sorority or a local book or garden club, be affiliated with a religious group, join a church, become a member of a seniors club, be selected for traveling sports teams, etc.

The tribal effect is why the political groups such as the Republicans, Democrats, Independents, and the Tea Party exist. Even though voting citizens are all officially called U.S. citizens and there is little logic to fussing, fighting, arguing, and debating with each other, people are still prone to join political groups. The yearning to be part of a team or tribe that competes against other teams or tribes is what unfortunately makes many people function and find a certain cause or purpose in life. This helps explain why so many religious denominations exist yet believe in the same two, three, or four basic principles. We yearn to compete, compare, and often gloat that we are part of a better or more-enlightened tribe or group of people.

This concept manifests itself in many aspects of life, ranging from families who believe they have better pedigrees than other families, to people living on one particular side of the "tracks" thinking they are superior to those on the other side. The tribal nature influences much of our society once you step back and examine the opposing beliefs behind more groups: union versus nonunion, management versus labor, clergy versus laypeople, and evangelicals versus orthodox, and this continues all the way down to the primitive level of street gangs.

Members of tribes have the tendency to make themselves wannabes and look-alikes with people they want to look like, act like, and be part of. The key aspect is to feel familiar with or like the tribe, team, or group because familiarity brings security and a sense of normalcy. When people feel they are part of a tribe, they sense they are like other people and can relax and be themselves, and in some cases they feel they can let go of their inhibitions. This is the reason why people in the same group or tribe start acting, modeling, patterning, and even looking like each other after they associate with each other long enough.

The desire for divorce may also be attributed to the tribal idea in that we grow apart and in essence see ourselves as part of another tribe, marriage, or family. Think of the stories of couples having reached certain points in their relationships and made one of the following statements:

+ We've just grown apart over the years!
+ I don't think I love you anymore!
+ Now that the kids are grown and gone, I think it's time we go our separate ways!
+ I should have told you years ago that I had feelings for my gender!
+ I don't know when it all started, but I've fallen in love with a younger person!

In each of these cases a portion of the excuses are really statements that say they envision themselves in a different relationship or tribe rather than the tribe they are presently a part of. Even though one person is usually devastated in these situations, the other desires to join a different relationship, and this overpowers and overrides the painful emotions he or she is creating for the other person.

In many of these situations those who depart want to go back to their original tribes after two years or so because they realize they had false perceptions of who they wanted to hang out with. Many come back to their senses and realize that the original tribal relationship they had was not that bad after all. Two years is generally the time it takes for emotional change and any false perceptions to wear off. Unfortunately, after two years it is hard to go back to a former relationship because the other person or people have moved on.

Normalcy Perceived through Microtribes

The social media craze combined with reality television has helped drive behaviors and ideas of what is normal to a whole new level. Within social media groups, people who have certain inklings of what is normal can find a social media group or gathering for just about any type of fad, trend, or pattern of behavior imaginable. If I want to start or find a group of hairy-legged kayakers I could probably do so quickly and start communicating as if we were a great tribe with a great purpose in life (no offense to hairy-legged kayakers)! Or if I wanted to find a group of women who are over forty-five years old and have birthed twins through Caesarian sections I'm sure I could do so.

The tribal effect is also a reason reality television shows that represent a slice of a society or tribe have become so popular. Who would have imagined there would be television shows representing antique pickers, pawn shops, truck drivers on icy roads, trading spouses, the biggest losers trying to lose weight, dancing with the stars, reality shows with large families such as the Duggar family, and even Dog the Bounty Hunter. Well over fifty reality television shows have covered many walks of life that represent tribes of some sort. This is all a way to make more people feel normal no matter how few people in the world really do what they do.

Reality television is a genre of programming that presents unscripted dramatic or humorous situations or documents actual events; it usually features ordinary people instead of professional actors. It lets us feel as if we are all ordinary people doing a combination of ordinary yet extraordinary things at the same time. We all enjoy seeing real people stumbling and processing life as we do. We have created a new level of perceived normalcy by creating microtribes of people who appear like we do. As humans we are trying to remedy the old feeling that we are not normal by changing the playing field of how normal is defined by connecting with others like us through television or the Internet. In many ways this has helped some people feel normal and take away the pressure of everyone trying to be the same "normal."

A Spiritual Shift: Up to the Level of Angels

Imagine what would happen if we could rise to a new level and actually see and act like the spiritual beings God created us to become? What if we actually believed the spiritual world was for our pleasure as well as God's good pleasure? What if our reality became a spiritual or higher reality we could start believing, seeing, and manifesting? For instance, if God told us we were born to do great things and we started seeing them through visions, imagination, faith, prayer, or meditation, we might start manifesting the behaviors that are being visualized through our imaginations, prayers, visions, dreams, etc.

Ephesians 3:18–21 encourages us to do exactly what you just read:

> I pray also that the eyes of your heart may be enlightened in order that you may know the hope to which he has called you, the riches of his glorious inheritance in the saints, and to know this love that surpasses knowledge—that you may be filled to the measure of all the fullness of God. Now to him who is able to do immeasurably more than all we ask or imagine, according to his power that is at work within us, to him be glory in the church and in Christ Jesus throughout all generations, for ever and ever! Amen.

According to this scripture passage, we are strongly encouraged to imagine and ask according to the power that works within us in order to see everything God has for us. Evidently we need less time on reality television and more time on imaging the greater things that could happen in life as we dream, imagine, and begin to walk out the greater things of God.

This concept of seeing and believing we are every bit as spiritual as we are physical is what Heaven 3.0 is all about: seeing the potential of heavenly realms with heavenly beings. What if I started seeing, believing, and desiring that I could be part of a spiritual tribe that could partake in supernatural activities? What if my longing were to leave the earthly nature of competitive tribes and experience the peace, power, and tranquility of heavenly thoughts and actions that change my personal world as well as the world around me for the better? In order to do this I would need to change my perception, shift my reference points, and set my sights on the highest common denominator.

According to scripture, the higher denominators are heavenly but do work between heaven and earth. In the Lord's Prayer we are asked to pray that God's will for us in heaven be accomplished on earth as well. Jesus tells us in Matthew 16:19 that He has given us the keys to the kingdom of God and that whatever we bind on earth will be bound in heaven and whatever we loose on earth will be loosed in heaven. We are given a lot of authority on God's behalf to facilitate things between heaven and earth! However, if I can't see this authority or don't desire it, I may never see the sides of heaven that were given for us to see and interact with.

If I want this authority and claim this authority, I am making a claim or statement that I want to be part of the heavenly host or tribe. When I start acting like a host of heaven or member of this tribe, I start seeing things that average people don't get to see. This concept is no different than a member of a gang or tribe on the streets of New York getting to see things the average person doesn't get to see; it's just that one sees heavenly things and the other sees earthly things.

Our Assignment Matches that of Angels— We Are of the Same Tribe

The type of authority we have been granted is the same kind of assignment or authority angels have. The word "angel" comes from the Greek word *aggelos*, which means "messenger." The matching Hebrew word *mal'ak* has the same meaning. This indicates that we as well as angels are God's messengers to help facilitate things between heaven and earth. As part of the same tribe of hosts or heavenly focused beings we naturally would be like other group members and help each other out in times of need. Yes, this indicates that we can minister to angels and angels can minister to us. The simple act of faith can be understood by reading the following scripture passages:

Do not forget to entertain strangers, for by so doing some people have entertained angels without knowing it. (Hebrews 13:2)

But the angel of the Lord by night opened the prison doors, and brought them forth, and said, go, stand and speak in the temple to the people all the words of this life. (Acts 5:19–20)

In Psalm 103, people as well as angels are referred to as God's host who do His good pleasure.

Bless the LORD, you His angels, who excel in strength, who do His word, heeding the voice of His word. Bless the LORD, all you His hosts, you ministers of His, who do His pleasure. (Psalm 103:20–21, NKJV)

You may never have been presented this type of teaching, yet it is the very teaching found in scripture. Many types and styles of biblical teaching are unintentionally trying to keep us separated from heavenly things on earth by following rules or commandments only. We are often trained to wait until some day in the future after we have earned the right or passage into heaven. However, this is untrue, as we cannot earn but only believe and see what has been promised. We are immediately grafted and given passage into God's family upon the very mention of salvation, Jesus's name.

When Jesus hears us confess and accept Him, His voice echoes that we have been initiated and given full privileges into the family of God. This simple act of confession and acceptance takes about ten seconds, after which we are born again. Upon being born again we are brought back to the rightful place of being created in God's image. With Jesus being the supreme leader of the ultimate family or tribe, we are granted full access into the kingdom of God upon this acceptance. The tribal effect is broader than we think when we consider that we cannot become part of the heavenly hosts, tribes, or family of God without making a claim that we want to be like Jesus by accepting His act of sacrifice. His initiation is simple and profound at the same time.

This type of thinking may put the born-again experience in a whole new context for many people. All I had to do was confess that Jesus acted as the ultimate leader as He died for all humanity's sins and that He was risen from physical death and placed at the right hand of God the Father in heaven, where he intercedes and interacts on humanity's behalf. My simple act of faith with my mouth that He did what He said He did and He is where He says He is allows me instant, free access into his family/tribe along with the other hosts of heaven. Once initiated into this, I naturally but supernaturally start wanting to do the things of heaven, where Christ sits and reigns. This is the whole context of the verse we started with, Colossians 3:1–2: "Since, then, you have been raised with Christ, set your hearts on things above, where Christ is seated at the right hand of God. Set your minds on things above, not on earthly things."

Summary

From 2004 to 2011 my job required me to travel around the country. God was gracious in many ways during my trips, experiences, and outcomes. I would often share openly with my family about the heavenly appointments God arranged on planes, in hotels, and at work. They were often amazed at some of the stories yet more amazed I made it home safe every time based on my attention to detail and driving finesse (or lack thereof). I would often respond to their comments, "Now do you believe in angels?" With a smile I say that God keep angels employed when I travel!

The truth and facts of my travels were that I made a conscious decision to purposely keep my eyes more open to the spiritual happenings than to the physical happenings around me. This allowed many open doors of opportunity for me to share the good news and dialog with people. At the same time it allowed me to let God provide protection and provision and to help me through His ministering angels.

I must admit that my willingness to operate in this fashion did not happen right away. I had to come to the conclusion that the more I focused on my own ability to survive on the road, the more stressed I became. I had to be kindly reminded that God was in charge of my life, travels, family, and safety.

In a more profound manner the context of this chapter explains why the Star of David was shining in the sky while people were traveling to Bethlehem when Jesus was born, but only a few people saw the star. Most people had their eyes on the ground and on taxes while the wise men somehow looked up to heaven when they saw the Star of David, indicating that the Messiah, Jesus, had been born.

What tribe would you say you belong too? What does your tribe look like, act like, sound like, and talk like?

CHAPTER 2

THE DOOR HAS BEEN OPENED; WHY NOT TAKE A PEEK?

I had only heard about you before, but now I have seen you with my own eyes. I take back everything I said, and I sit in dust and ashes to show my repentance.

—Job 42:5–6 NLT

There are only two ways to live your life. One is as though nothing is a miracle. The other is as though everything is a miracle.

—Albert Einstein

On many of my flights I would ask business travelers, teenagers, and parents if they had had any dreams recently. The manner in which I asked the question was so casual that I would sort of ignore the fact that I even asked the question. Usually within an hour the person would ask, "Why did you ask me what I've been dreaming lately?" I would tell them I was just wondering, as I know people are having more dreams lately. This would spark a great conversation on dreams and their personal situations and allow me to ask, "Whose dreams were they?" They would reply "Mine. Why?" I would smile and conclude that God speaks through dreams as described in Job 33:14–18, and He desires your attention. I would also state that there was a national report in December 2008 stating over 1,000,000 people from the Middle East accepted Jesus through just one personal dream. (Please Google this fact by typing "Muslims come to Christ through dreams.")

The manner in which I openly held such impromptu discussions was quite simple, as I knew that the study of dreams within the field of science has proven that everyone dreams every night but not everyone remembers his or her dreams. In addition, God stated in the last days of church history that He would pour out His Spirit upon all flesh and everyone would start dreaming more frequently (Acts 2:17–20).

What I was attempting to accomplish during these subtle, non-confrontational, and informal discussions was to let people know that God had opened the doors of information, visions, dreams, and knowledge to all people. Considering that medical science has determined that dreams are beneficial and can solve problems and remedy issues, it is amazing more people do not openly endorse them. With God stating that He gives dreams (Job 33:14–18), and that they will be increased in the last days (Acts 2:17–18), it would appear that spiritual leaders are without excuse for not endorsing dreams and visions for solving spiritual problems.

Two relevant, modern-day news articles confirm that dreams are occurring on a worldwide scale:

+ *The American Mind Journal,* November/December 2011

issue front-page story was, "You Must Be Dreaming: Creatively Solving Your Problems While You Sleep."

+ *Charisma*, January 11, 2010 posted an article on charismatics entitled "Muslims Coming to Christ through Dreams, Visions, and Miracles." Within this posting was the following quotation:

"A tsunami of faith is quietly overtaking the Muslim world. Islamic adherents are laying aside their allegiance to Muhammad to follow Jesus Christ, despite the social ostracism, persecution and possible martyrdom that converts to Christianity face. Propelled by dreams, visions and miracles, this wave of revival is bringing vast numbers of Muslims—some say millions—into God's kingdom." Source: Charisma, January 11, 2010

What are the implications of just these two breakthroughs, let alone dozens of other breakthrough concepts? Below is just the tip of the iceberg on what it may indicate:

+ God's Word described in Daniel 12:4 is proving true when the archangel shared with Daniel that in the last days travel and knowledge would increase (Daniel 12:4).
+ Science and God's Word are starting to come together, which allows people to recognize that all knowledge, miracles, and revelations are God's.
+ Science is catching up with God, and therefore there are some "way cool" intersections of truth.
+ God's version of the Gospel is so personalized for individual people that God is willing to transfer it directly into the minds of individuals even though they live in areas where the Gospel can't be shared.
+ It implies that God will use human messengers to spread the Gospel, but He has direct and instant means that far surpass our methods, proving He doesn't need people, even though He is willing to use people to share the Gospel.
+ God is able to dump out, pour out, spread out, whisper out,

and dream out His visions, words, and knowledge to people in any manner He chooses and at any rate He chooses.

- A vivid dream of Christ and Christ crucified must be powerful enough and clear enough in a dream to help people confess His name for salvation.
- The fulfillment of the promise in Habakkuk 2:14 may be easily accomplished through various means. In fact, it could be accomplished in one evening: "For the earth will be filled with the knowledge of the glory of the LORD, as the waters cover the sea."

I trust you are grasping the concept of this chapter, titled "The doors are open; why not take a peek?" God has given the opportunity for every human being from every tribe, every tongue, and every nation to peek into the windows of heaven. When you peek through the windows and doorway of heaven you are guaranteed to see the things of heaven! We must move beyond the hearing of heaven and be as Job and see with our eyes the things of heaven so we can get the fullest view, experience, and blessing from heaven. We are in the days of Heaven 3.0!

Expanding a Peek into a Full View of Heavenly Things?

One of the simplest concepts I started learning to apply in my life was that I could accomplish what I visualized. I realized I was created by God to see His beauty, glory, power, honor, future, and possibilities through my life. The missing link was that in the past I had only heard of these possibilities, but suddenly I realized I needed to start seeing with my spiritual eyes. Read and think about the words penned by the fourteenth-century priest and writer Thomas à Kempis: "Those who attempt to search into the majesty of God will be overwhelmed with His Glory!" The following scripture passages helped me realize the concept of using my eyes to peek into the invisible and heavenly aspects of God.

> I pray also that the eyes of your heart may be enlightened in order that you may know the hope to which he has called you, the riches of his glorious inheritance in the saints. (Ephesians 1:18)

My ears had heard of you but now my eyes have seen you. (Job 42:5)

The eye is the lamp of the body. If your eyes are good, your whole body will be full of light. But if your eyes are bad, your whole body will be full of darkness. If then the light within you is darkness, how great is that darkness! (Matthew 6:22–23)

When I was a child, I talked like a child, I thought like a child, I reasoned like a child. When I became a man, I put childish ways behind me. Now we see but a poor reflection as in a mirror; then we shall see face to face. Now I know in part; then I shall know fully, even as I am fully known. (1 Corinthians 13:11–12)

Through scripture and my own experiences I realized that our minds, wills, and emotions are like magnets. Just like magnets, my mind, will, and emotions are pulled toward my visual curiosity. Wherever my eyes are focused draw my attention, mind, emotions, and heart. This is the simple concept explained in Matthew 6:21: "Where your treasure is, there will your heart be also." This simply means that whatever we are imagining or visioning, is really what is in our hearts, and therefore is where we will invest our thoughts, emotions, and energies.

The magnet field of my life is what I set my "eyes" upon. For instance, as a freshman in high school I won a track meet in the 800 meter and witnessed the feeling of breaking the winner's ribbon at the finish line, the crowd cheering, my teammates hollering positive words of encouragement, and the coach patting me on the back. This experience allowed me to invest the next four years setting my vision on breaking the school track record and reaching new levels of recognition. This vision was healthy, consuming, and rewarding from an athletic and peer perspective. However, the strength of my vision and passion caused me to miss the social and relational aspects of life for those four years of high school.

After high school and living in a community filled with both recreational and abusive alcoholism, I put my sights on catching up on social activities that gravitated around alcohol. For the next fifteen years my vision was set on the lower behavior patterns of drinking, fighting, arguing, and resenting who I had become. Seeing I was being drawn by animal-level magnetic pulls, I started doing what others at lower levels do, and I allowed my energies to pull me toward the desires of my lower-level nature. If I had been drawn to higher levels of heavenly and angelic thoughts, I would have started doing things of a higher order in life. Bishop Fulton Sheen figured this out and stated, "Each of us makes his own weather, determines the color of the skies, in the universe which we inhabit." Bishop Sheen was saying what we see is what we believe, so why not inhabit the highest realm of the universe God has allowed us to see?

When we seek heavenly things we start envisioning them and therefore enter a different space in time. This is the space in time when we start seeing heavenly places with our eyes and not just hearing about them with our ears. This was the very contrast that Jesus was telling Nicodemus about in John 3:12: "I have spoken to you of earthly things and you do not believe; how then will you believe if I speak of heavenly things?" Jesus was trying to create a universe in Nicodemus's mind that included heavenly, not just earthly, things.

In the fall of 1991 I tasted my last drop of alcohol and confessed the name of Jesus. On that particular Sunday in 1991, God came into my heart and life, and I started setting my sights on higher-level concepts that have brought me into realms of possibilities that I could never have imagined during my former life. Yes, that is correct—I found a new life in 1991 and started my magnetic pull toward heavenly thoughts, concerns, and ambitions. I recognized it was a new life as I saw things change in my mind, thoughts, and ambitions, but most of all there was the evidence that all my drinking friends left me, or I left them. My former friends and I each had different magnetic pulls on our destinies; they were being pulled one way, and I was being pulled a different way. They saw things I no longer wanted to see, and I saw things they could not yet see.

My new life became the best decision and vision I have ever made as well as decided to see. The verse "If any man be in Christ, He is a new creature, behold all old things are passed away and yes all things become new" (1 Corinthians 5:17) was fully activated in my life. I love the fact that the Bible passage uses the word "creature" because I went from a lower-level "monkey see monkey do" mindset into the realm of the "angel see angel do" mindset. In a split second I went from an animal-based creature to a heavenly creature. It took me thirty years of hardship to make this split-second decision before I switched tribes, and I have never looked back again.

On that same Sunday in 1991 my wife, Pam, got out of the caged world she had been living in as well. She left behind the lower-level creature behavior and entered into heavenly behavior. As new heavenly creatures we found a new life and new marriage and are now on our twenty-fifth year of marriage.

It took me thirty years to see things clearly and switch my habitat of lower-level living. This thirty-year journey makes me appreciate how one dream can change a person from one religious belief into a Christian overnight. This type of change in our world is the life-changing power of heaven opening up in a quicker and broader fashion. People who have had a dream and believed it must have gotten the full glimpse of heaven and bypassed the "peeking" that Pam and I had done for thirty years.

The simple concept of our vision being just like a magnetic field that pulls us toward what we set our eyes on affects all aspects of how we perceive our universe. Seeing produces results, and our results produce our direction, and our direction produces our belief, and our belief produces our destiny, and our destiny defines our fate. This concept works in all walks of life. This is why alcoholics seek out other drinkers, taverns, and liquor stores and why drug users seek out the places where drugs are sold and parties where like-minded people hang out.

On a more positive note, this concept is also representative of great golfers, bowlers and other athletes, speakers, preachers, etc. They set their sights on winning and therefore hang out in places where winners are trained and coached. Take any habit, profession, hobby, or attitude in life and you will find that people who see the same kind of things, think the same way, act the same way, and talk the same way find each other, proving that we copy one another and are magnetically pulled toward each other according to what we see.

God continues to crack open the door into many aspects of life, including heavenly realms, which are realms that allow bidirectional communication, where people see angels and Jesus and witness miracles and healings that intersect heaven and earth.

Examples of Heaven and Earth Meeting

During the May 2011 Joplin, Missouri tornado, many children reported seeing angels and also stated that they even saw who they believed was Jesus walking with them during the darkest hours of the tornado. Many stories and books have been written about these types of experiences. What is happening is fairly simple: when people are put in a unique circumstance such as car accidents, tornadoes, surgeries, or other near-death experiences, they suddenly have their senses recalibrated and closely aligned with heavenly things. The closer they get toward the edges of this physical life the less they see the lower physical realm and find themselves reaching to heavenly realms for solutions. This is truly the place where heaven meets earth. People in these situations suddenly see images of heavenly things as if they were partners with heavenly beings. Up until that moment of despair or need these individuals have only heard about these types of experiences or sightings, but suddenly, as Job, they see the reality of what they heard about. They have entered a new realm of understanding about heaven. They are no longer limited to the Heaven 1.0 they saw in a movie or read about in a book. Upon their sightings of heavenly things they now believe they are part of the tribe (hosts) of heavenly beings. They have graduated beyond the many people who choose to view earth as an entity separate from heaven.

These experiences create a complete reversal of a "monkey see monkey do" mindset, making it an "angel see angel do" matter. These people start believing they are truly part of a new tribe of heavenly hosts. This is why people who have experienced things like this start to write books and often go on speaking tours. Their new visions, lives, and purposes become so magnetizing that they must tell the world about the doors opened to them. A few examples of these individuals include:

- *90 Minutes in Heaven: A True Story of Death and Life* by Don Piper and Cecil Murphey.
- *The Boy Who Came Back from Heaven: A Remarkable Account of Miracles, Angels, and Life beyond This World* by Kevin Malarkey and Alex Malarkey.
- *Heaven is for Real: A Little Boy's Astounding Story of His Trip to Heaven and Back* by Todd Burpo.

These individuals were in circumstances that helped them see through the open door into the heavenly realms. This is the place where there is a miraculous interchange between heaven and earth. Seeing heavenly things does not make heaven more or less real; heaven, God, Jesus, the Holy Spirit, and their heavenly hosts are constantly present, real, and accessible. These experiences allow them to make different decisions, prepare for life through new lenses, and enjoy life differently than if they had never had the experience. Geraldine Berkheimer says the following about the impact of her heavenly experience: "Although my near death experience was nearly thirty-four years ago, there is virtually not a day that goes by that I am not aware of making decisions based on that experience."

The facts are clear that God has opened the doors of heaven far and wide when Jesus was sacrificed, as explained vividly in Colossians and Galatians. He nailed everything to the cross and opened up the universe by transcending time and space when he traveled from the depths to the heights of existence (time) and the universe (space). Review the following scriptural passages and imagine that the boundaries we have placed on ourselves have been removed and the doors have been opened for all people who believe and accept the greatest travel agent of all time, Jesus. He took the first flight to the depths and the heights and has now opened the doors for all frequent fliers to travel.

Entering into this fullness is not something you figure out or achieve. It's not a matter of being circumcised or keeping a long list of laws. No, you're already in—insiders—not through some secretive initiation rite but rather through what Christ has already gone through for you, destroying the power of sin. If it's an initiation ritual you're after, you've already been through it by submitting to baptism. Going under the water was a burial of your old life; coming up out of it was a resurrection, God raising you from the dead as he did Christ. When you were stuck in your old sin-dead life, you were incapable of responding to God. God brought you alive—right along with Christ! Think of it! All sins forgiven, the slate wiped clean, that old arrest warrant canceled and nailed to Christ's cross. He stripped all the spiritual tyrants in the universe of their sham authority at the Cross and marched them naked through the streets. (Colossians 2:11–15 Message Version)

When he ascended on high, he led captives in his train and gave gifts to men. What does "he ascended" mean except that he also descended to the lower, earthly regions? He who descended is the very one who ascended higher than all the heavens, in order to fill the whole universe. (Ephesians 4:8-10 NIV)

He climbed the high mountain, He captured the enemy and seized the booty, He handed it all out in gifts to the people. It's true, is it not, that the One who climbed up also climbed down, down to the valley of earth? And the One who climbed down is the One who climbed back up, up to highest heaven. He handed out gifts above and below, filled heaven with his gifts. (Ephesians 4:8–10 Message Version).

These passages and many more indicate we do not need to go through extreme circumstances to experience what God has already prepared and given us; all we need to do is allow our minds to image we are not separated from heaven but included in heaven. This is God's promise! We have the opportunity to expand our imaginations, thoughts, experiences, and happenings to include the things of the kingdom of God and heaven.

We no longer need to wait for impossible ordeals, circumstances, or life-or-death moments to see heavenly things. Jesus told his disciples to pray that God's will be done on earth as it is in heaven; in other words, we can pray and then start seeing the will of God in heaven so that it becomes reality on earth. This simple belief was exactly what happened in the dreams of Daniel, Solomon, Abraham, Joseph, Mary and Joseph,

Paul, Peter, John, and numerous others. They saw heavenly activities in dreams and visions and then walked them out to be fulfilled on earth. Let's look at three examples:

1. Peter had a vision in which he saw heaven open up with a sheet draping down heaven with all kinds of unclean animals. The vision as told in Acts 10–12 was the clear evidence that allowed Gentiles to be accepted into heaven. Even though Peter debated in his mind about the vision that was instantaneously given three times, he finally agreed that God's vision must be turned into reality. He went to the house of Cornelius, who also had a vision about sending for Peter (Acts 10:4–7) to come share Christ with them. After Cornelius's household received salvation, Peter had to go and address the leaders of the Church in Jerusalem and rationalize with them that all Gentiles were then welcome into the kingdom simply based on His vision of a sheet coming down from heaven with four unclean animals and the experience with Cornelius.

    Peter had to walk out on earth the very will of God that was determined in his vision from heaven. Peter lived and walked out the part of the Lord's Prayer, which states "that God's will in heaven be done on earth."

2. King Solomon, the wisest man in the world, was but a young teenager when he took over as king for his father David. In 1 Kings 3:5–15 we read that God appeared to this young man in a dream in which God asked Solomon what he wanted from God. Within the dream, Solomon replied that he wanted wisdom above all else. God replied that he would be given wisdom, and because he asked for wisdom instead of wealth, He would also be given wealth. When Solomon awoke he had to determine if he would walk out the promise of God from heaven on earth. As the story goes, Solomon believed and received the dream as a key message from God and got everything that was promised here in this lifetime.

3. Joseph and Mary were saved by a dream. When Jesus was born,

53

King Herod was furious that the wise men never came back to tell him where Jesus had been born. King Herod ordered the killing of all boys two years and younger throughout the region. At that same time an angel came to Joseph in a dream and told him to get up and get Jesus and Mary out of the region and into Egypt. Matthew 2:1–23 states that Joseph immediately woke up and got a U-Haul and went to Egypt. Okay, it was not a U-Haul but a U-Camel.

These three examples are just a few of the 160 times dreams are used in scripture. Many of the dreams and visions were life-changing dreams from heaven that had to be walked out on earth. Dreams are visual, but they must be received and believed in order for the dreamer to get the passion, desire, and tenacity to start walking them out on earth. In this sense "seeing" and "envisioning" are often the starting point for walking out faith.

The simple concept of being drawn like magnets to what we visualize applies in the supernatural, spiritual walks of life. If I see, talk, walk, read, and behave like a heavenly being created by God, I will eventually find others who do the same. And through this process some of these people will be found in a heavenly realm where heavenly people hang out.

The Apostle Paul shared a few examples in the Bible of people who experienced the joys of entering heavenly realms and communicating with people. Many times heavenly minded people cannot always distinguish the difference between heavenly and earthly things; they often walk between heavenly and earthly realms without knowing. On the other hand, maybe they are just walking out God's heavenly will on earth, which is one and the same for them. Many of these people have been accused of wrongdoing, and people tell them "Pull your head out of the clouds!" An example is in Acts 12:7–9, where Peter interacted with an angel and did not know if it was a vision or dream or really happening: "Suddenly an angel of the Lord appeared and a light shone in the cell. He struck Peter on the side and woke him up. 'Quick, get up!' he said, and the chains fell off Peter's wrists. Then the angel said to him, 'Put on your clothes and sandals.' And Peter did so. 'Wrap your cloak around you and follow me,' the angel told him. Peter followed him out of the prison, but he had no idea that what the angel was doing was really happening; he thought he was seeing a vision." This same type of experience happens on a regular basis when the need and desire to visualize heavenly things arise.

Seeing and experiencing the kingdom of God on earth are the very reasons great men and women of God seek out places where God is heard about, including synagogues, churches, etc., but also includes places invisible to the normal, physical eye, places in the spiritual realm that are sensed through visions, dreams, prayers, and imagined as visualized and believed scripture. Throughout scripture, the percentage of time great men and women of God spent in a building was far less than the time they spent in places where they experienced the presence, visitation, and/or manifestation of God all by themselves. The reason is simply because many people are not looking for the omnipresence of God in ordinary ways or are too busy fussing about life that they can't see what is right in front of them. The prime example and proof of this is the story of Cleopas and his counterpart found in Luke 13:33. Cleopas and his counterpart were walking around after Jesus was crucified, fussing over the whole ordeal. Jesus walked up to them in His resurrected body, but they had no idea who He was: "Jesus kept them from recognizing Him." He kept them from recognizing Him because of their tone of voice and discussion about the events of His death. The passage mentions that they were downcast and looking down, not up. Jesus intentionally withheld himself from being seen by them because they were focused and fussing about the half-truth that Jesus was dead, while the fact was that He had been dead but was at that point alive. He was seen immediately by other people who saw Jesus's resurrected body and believed.

To experience the heavenly realms of possibility we must be looking or at least peeking into the realms of heaven. It is one thing to hear about heavenly things but a whole new thing to start experiencing the things of heaven.

The doors are open. Are you peeking, staring, and setting your expectations, imaginations, and desires on things that are in heaven in order to walk out heaven on earth?

COMING OUT OF THE CLOSET: THE FACTS ARE ON GOD'S SIDE

I have spoken to you of earthly things and you do not believe; how then will you believe if I speak of heavenly things?

—John 3:12

We are not merely physical beings trying to grasp the spiritual and heavenly realm; rather we are spiritual and heavenly beings passing through an earthly and physical realm. What makes this is a fact is that we were created in the image of a spiritual and heavenly Father!

—Michael L. Mathews

In Jesus's discourse with Nicodemus in John chapter 3 (please read), Jesus was desperately trying to explain heavenly and spiritual truths to Nicodemus, a religious leader. Unfortunately, as both a religious leader and educated person Nicodemus was locked into the physical, educational, and earthy realm of understanding, so Jesus left him with mostly earthly thoughts even though He wanted to bring Nicodemus to his spiritual and heavenly birth and nature.

It is critical to note that Nicodemus started the conversation recognizing that Jesus must be from heaven (God) because no one else could do these types of signs and wonders unless God was with Him (John 3:1–2). Upon Nicodemus's confession that Jesus was from heaven, Jesus immediately attempted to bring Nicodemus up to the spiritual, heavenly level. Unfortunately, due to his years of living, learning, and clinging to the earthly realm of understanding, Nicodemus was not able to receive and enter into this heavenly realm. This is known because Nicodemus was one of the people who attempted to perform an earthly burial after Jesus's death, indicating that he understood the earthly nature of Jesus but did not comprehend the spiritual and heavenly resurrection of Jesus's body, which would not need to be prepared for an earthly burial (John 10:39–40).

Why did Jesus try so hard to get Nicodemus to see the realms of the kingdom, believe in it, and enter into it in Nicodemus's present life and future eternal life? I believe the answer is simple: God desires to bring each of us back to and through our "true" creation, which is more heavenly and spiritual than earthly. Jesus knows that when He is able to stretch our realms of earthly understanding and we grasp the spiritual realms of the kingdom, we will never want to limit ourselves to the earthly and physical world that binds so many.

One of the main reasons I believe that Jesus became the incarnate Christ (came in the flesh) and passed through the earthly body of Mary was to grasp and comprehend why humans cannot easily escape the feeling of being so earthly and human. Ever since the creation of humanity we have been given spiritual creations (births). Jesus knew that humanity was originally created in the spiritual realm in the image and likeness of God's nature, which is spiritual and heavenly. This is why God knew each of us before we were born in the earthly realm. It is God's spiritual birth for humanity that makes the perfect and spiritual birth first. Adam and Eve sinned after humanity was created in God's perfect image, so we must come back to understand this birth so God receives the credit. This view of creation may have been the very essence of the message of "being born again" that Nicodemus could not grasp.

> *Jesus knows that if he can stretch our realms of earthly understanding and we grasp the spiritual realms of the kingdom, we will never want to limit ourselves to the physical boundaries that the earthly and physical world have bound so many people into.*

We are first and foremost (from the beginning of time) given a spiritual birth because of our creation in the image of God (Genesis 1:26–27). Giving credit to my earthly mother and father before my spiritual father is spiritually out of order. How can I be so sure about this? The Bible states that Christ Jesus was the firstborn of every creature both visible and invisible (Colossians 1:15). Because Christ was the firstborn of the creature, the creation, called humanity, and we are created in His image, then we were connected to His spiritual birth before we were born to our earthly parents. Jesus was a key component of the "let us create man in our image" because He was the firstborn of every idea and creation God had.

Unfortunately, because our first earthly memories have us processed through earthly bodies to be born into an earthly environment, we are prone to see earth as our first and primary kingdom instead of the combined kingdoms of heaven and earth. This is why so many people remain "earthy" and completely blot out their true reflections in God, or spiritual birth. This concept is exactly what Jesus was attempting to get Nicodemus to see in John chapter 3: "You must confess and acknowledged that you can be born again in order to see and enter the fullness of the kingdom." If we can't see and believe we were first and foremost a spiritual creation of God we will never be able to walk or enter into the spiritual kingdom! Through this story Jesus was trying to help Nicodemus and all humans comprehend that they were first and foremost spiritual beings created in God's image and through the image of the firstborn of all creation, Jesus. If they confess this simple truth, they can come back to that perfect image and be born again.

God spoke: "Let us make human beings in our image, make them reflecting our nature so they can be responsible for the fish in the sea, the birds in the air, the cattle, and, yes, Earth itself, and every animal that moves on the face of Earth." God created human beings; he created them godlike, reflecting God's nature. He created them male and female." (Genesis 1:26–27 MSG)

This is what the LORD says—your redeemer, who formed you in the womb: I am the LORD, who has made all things, who alone stretched out the heavens, who spread out the earth by myself. (Isaiah 44:24)

Before I formed you in the womb I knew you, before you were born I set you apart; I appointed you as a prophet to the nations. (Jeremiah 1:5)

For you created my inmost being; you knit me together in my mother's womb. (Psalm 139:13)

Your eyes saw my unformed body. All the days ordained for me were written in your book before one of them came to be. (Psalm 139:16)

This may sound strange, but it is the reason Jesus stated the process in the words found in Matthew 6:33: "Seek you first the kingdom of God and His righteousness and then everything else will follow." If I seek the kingdom of God, which includes my spiritual birth, then all the other things will follow. This is the proper sequence in which my life becomes ordered of God. Doing the opposite is why so many individuals, people, families, and tribes struggle with earthly relationships.

Jesus's hope is that people would see, enter, and believe in the heavenly realm as much as they do the earthly realm. Jesus was trying to make it so simple that all we have to do is accept and confess this spiritual birth (again) and thus be born back into it (born again). This understanding was proven by Christ coming through the earthly birthing process and reversing creation back to its original spiritual order.

We are capable of being born again through Jesus, who is called the second Adam (heavenly Adam), and have come through the earthly birthing process to set the record straight. Christ's earthly birth gives the right of passage into the heavenly realms if we can believe (see) in our first spiritual birth through Christ. This concept is the essence of these scripture passages:

> And just as we have borne the likeness of the earthly man, so shall we bear the likeness of the man from heaven. (1 Corinthians 15:49)

> God knew what he was doing from the very beginning. He decided from the outset to shape the lives of those who love him along the same lines as the life of his Son. The Son stands first in the line of humanity he restored. We see the original and intended shape of our lives there in him. (Romans 8:28 MSG)

> Do not lie to each other, since you have taken off your old self with its practices and have put on the new self, which is being renewed in knowledge in the image of its Creator. (Colossians 3:9–10)

> All of us! Nothing between us and God, our faces shining with the brightness of his face. And so we are transfigured much like the Messiah, our lives gradually becoming brighter and more beautiful as God enters our lives and we become like him. (2 Corinthians 3:18 MSG)

Jesus came out of the closet for every human being and gives our spiritual birth back again; therefore we can be born again into the spiritual state whereby we can start to see and enter the spiritual kingdom. This is why Jesus says we do not belong to the world any more than He belongs to the world (John 17:16).

Nicodemus was getting confused because his earthly realm of possibility was not elastic enough to expand into the spiritual realm; he could never see the fullness of the spiritual kingdom even though it had already been given to all humanity. All he had to do was confess this simple heavenly principle (or should I say believe).

Jesus reversed His birthing process of being born in heaven and came through the earthly process, just like you and me. He performed the ultimate miracle for each of us so we can see, believe, and enter the kingdom and see the signs and wonders of God, heaven, and the kingdom of God. This whole concept is really that simple, but this can make it difficult to comprehend. Unfortunately, by the time Jesus revealed this simple truth to Nicodemus he was brainwashed, overeducated, and locked into earthly ignorance to the point that the spiritual birthing process was almost impossible for him to accept.

Even though Jesus said that reclaiming the spiritual birth, being born again, was this simple, Nicodemus would not believe this new, earthly concept. Because he could not believe, he could not see, and because he could not see, he could not enter the kingdom as Jesus described. Like many of us, Nicodemus chose to stay on the earthly playing field of life. This whole process is described in Figure 3.1.

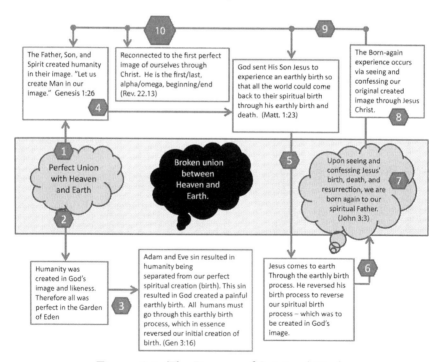

Figure 3.1: The Process of Spiritual Birth

God took Jesus's earthly birth one step further by arranging it in a manger among earthly animals. Who would ever be able to argue a true earthly birth considering it took place in a manger among earthly creatures? Jesus could now relate and identify to the strong sense of being pasteurized, processed, birthed, and born through an earthly vessel. In modern-day language He came out of the closet in a big way.

By Jesus completing this process of coming from the heavenly realm to the earthly realm, He literally flips our earthly process 180 degrees by allowing us to be reprocessed from an earthly birth to a heavenly birth, a new birth or born again. His desire is to have us identify, share, communicate, and enter back into the heavenly realm by being pasteurized back again to the perfect image whereby we were originally created. This is why Jesus was called the Son of Man and the Son of God and the "door." Jesus became the open door by which humanity could pass back and forth. The earthly realm and heavenly realm were connected in a fresh way, thus the kingdom of God includes heaven and earth, and we are told to seek first the kingdom of God (Matthew 6:33).

> I am the door. If anyone enters by Me, he will be saved, and will go in and out and find pasture. (John 10:9 NKJV)

Pasteurization is the process whereby a substance is heated to a high temperature to kill bacteria. You may think this metaphor sounds strange, but listen to Job 10:10: "Did you not pour me out like milk and curdle me like cheese?" Job was brought through a cleansing process to kill all foreign objects in himself. In the same manner Jesus was brought through the process of human birth and killed all our sins, even though He Himself knew no sin. He reversed the process of us being cleansed by experiencing human birth even though He was God. The phrase that can best describe this is "reverse pasteurized," a way by which He completed the entire rebirth for all humanity and in that process removed all roadblocks to God, wiping away all past sins and future sins for anyone who confesses this simple process. He removed the crud of all earthly things by coming through the earthly process. Jesus came from heaven through a fleshly birth to identify with our earthly nature, and now He wants us to come back again through His spiritual birth (ours from the beginning) so we can identify with His spiritual nature.

When God created the human race, he created it in his image. When it was time to bring back the human race to that original birth, He did it once for all humanity. For God so loved the entire human race that He gave His Son for everyone to be part of the heavenly family of God through being born back into our original image, that of God. The only requirement is confessing the process and method. Now that you know the process was Jesus and the method was His birth, death, and resurrection, everyone can be born again upon that confession (John 3:16; Romans 10:9–10).

John 3 makes it even clearer that Jesus wanted so desperately for Nicodemus to come out of his earthly closet so Jesus could share heavenly things with him. Unfortunately, Nicodemus believed like many of today's earthly vessels who are institutionalized to a system of earthly means. Nicodemus seemed to believe that if we are too heavenly minded we will be no earthly good. The sad, often repeated quotation "That we can be so heavenly minded, that we will be of no earthly good," is a tragic statement that has robbed many people from seeing their true creation, their Creator, and their personal potential through their spiritual Creator. The enemy has fooled them just like he fooled Adam and Even into thinking that earthly fruit is more valuable than heavenly fruit. This lie, this fallacy has kept far too many people in the closet and focused on earthly things instead of heavenly things.

Over 2,000 years ago Jesus came out of the heavenly closet and opened up the truth that we can all come out of the earthly closet through His heavenly door (Jesus Himself) and have a heavenly life simply by being reconnected to our spiritual birth. Sad but true, there are still millions of people who have not seen and confessed this simple truth. Without seeing it they cannot receive this truth; it is hidden from them, even though it is right before their very eyes (Luke 13:13).

God is starting to reveal heavenly realms of the kingdom for people to see the fuller reflection of His truth, and the truth is that the kingdom of God is real. Jesus was doing nothing more than opening the door out of the religious, earthly closet Nicodemus wanted to hide in. As a reminder, Nicodemus came to Jesus quietly and in the evening hours by himself because he did not want to come out of the closet (John 3:1).

Jesus was indeed the door or entry way that would have allowed Nicodemus out of the closet of religion and into the heavenly realm. This is the reason Jesus referred to Himself as the entry way in these passages:

> I tell you the truth, the man who does not enter the sheep pen by the gate, but climbs in by some other way, is a thief and a robber. (John 10:1)

> Jesus answered, "I am the way and the truth and the life. No one comes to the Father except through me." (John 14:6)

> Here I am! I stand at the door and knock. If anyone hears my voice and opens the door, I will come in and eat with him, and he with me. (Revelation 3:20)

These are clear indicators who the door is. In addition, Jesus is the door and stands at the door and waits for you and me to take the initiative and knock. As soon as we knock, we confess that we believe He is the door and the passage out of the earthly closet into greater realms of forgiveness, understanding, authority, and the kingdom of God. Upon this confession, this knock, we can walk out of our earthly closet and enter His kingdom. This is why Jesus states He is willing to give us the keys to the kingdom whereby we have a living area much larger than the earthly closet we often stay within.

> I will give you the keys of the kingdom of heaven; whatever you bind on earth will be bound in heaven, and whatever you loose on earth will be loosed in heaven. (Matthew 16:19)

For any of us to come out of our closet of dysfunction, addiction, guilt, shame, insecurity, religion, poverty, and so on, we must go through the door to the heavenly realm that was provided by Jesus and reconnect with the our human birth of being created in God's image. This brings me to a very personal coming out of the closet for Pam and I, which allowed us to start seeing what we classify as Heaven 3.0. In 2010 we started seeing the heavenly realms we had only read about. The reason we could not see them was simply because we were behind curtains and closets of religion that allowed us to see only what we had been taught, but now we can see what God promised in 1 Corinthians 2:9–10: "Eye hath not seen nor ear heard, neither has entered into the heart of man the things God has prepared for those who love Him." Up until that point we had experienced what religion, churches, pastors, cell groups, study groups, Bible groups, and buddy groups had prepared for us. Suddenly we started seeing and believing the things that God had prepared for us.

Mike and Pam's Coming Out of the Closet

In January 2007 Pam and I started speaking up and out about the number of times that God used clouds as a means of communication, travel, or meetings. During one of the first services we delivered this subtle message a prophetic word came forth: *I desire and long for each of you to enter my realm of possibility.* Pam and I knew our facts were accurate because we were using scripture and referencing the over 200 times clouds are mentioned in scripture, yet we still felt that we should speak in a rather "what if" manner of talk versus a "matter of fact" manner of talk. As an example we would suddenly insert comments into the sermon/message such as:

- Did I mention that God delivered the Ten Commandments to Moses in the clouds?
- Did I mention that clouds serve as God's chariot?
- Did I mention that the Lord Jesus went up in the clouds and will also return in the clouds?
- Did I mention that the voice that said "This is My Son with whom I am well pleased" came from a cloud?
- Did I mention that the Israelites were led by a cloud by day and a pillar of fire by night?

We would intentionally integrate these comments into the sermon/message as a means not to appear that we were preaching what some would have labeled heresy. We were sure not to make any claims, define doctrine, or theology about clouds as we knew we would be breaking the appropriate Heaven 1.0 type of doctrinal protocol. Even in 2007 it was risky business talking crazy by saying things such as God could move in forms outside of Heaven 1.0 doctrine or the confines of church, even though the Bible mentions it numerous times.

After speaking engagements in 2007 in California, Missouri, and Wisconsin, we suddenly started receiving emails and calls after the sermons in which we had included subtle biblical statements on clouds. The emails and calls were all extremely enlightening and proof that ministers can come out of the closet when prompted. Below is just one of the excerpts from the ministers who started coming out of the closet.

> Mike, I noticed you slipped into your message some concepts about clouds. I was shocked you did that because for a few years now I have been having visions about clouds. In these visions I was actually meeting my deceased wife in the clouds. I am serious! I have been having these crazy visions that I could not share with anyone because they would think I was crazy. When you shared those passages, I was so blessed and shocked … and maybe I am not crazy after all.

Many more comments came from ministers and listeners as we started slowly leaking out the abstract concepts of God that have always been in scripture. The problem has been and will continue to be that earthy people do not see heavenly concepts very easily. They may be right in the Bible, but "earthy" means building churches, raising money, and counting heads, and this works against their ability to see spiritual things. This process of coming out of our earthly realms for Pam and me included sharing how the many increased and bizarre weather patterns that started around 2006 were merely nature's way of responding to God's voice. Our experiences led to writing a book on dreams that shared over thirty significant biblical dreams whereby doctrine has been defined in a spiritual manner.

During 2007, after writing on what appeared by many to be abstract concepts of scripture, we started getting many eyebrows raised at us. In fact, after our second book on dreams came out, we were told by many friends that their pastors advised them to stop hanging around a heretic such as myself. We realized that the abstract concepts we were teaching were very scriptural, but you can't build a business, social gathering, or modern-day church on them. Clergy leaders would lose control of gatherings at which everyone was starting to have dreams and visions that appear to be of God. Worse yet, if people did something about their dreams, the franchised church denominations would not work as earthly minds have designed them, and they may lose their positions, buildings, and standings within the franchise. One of the very reasons God may have decided to use dreams in an increased manner in the last days is that dreams would become the universal language that no church or denomination could claim ownership of.

In 2007, after testing the waters of our writings on the biblical aspects of clouds, weathers, dreams, calamities, delusions, heaven, and so on, we decided to write to an acquaintance of one of the world's largest denominations on just the weather concept. I made sure I used 100 percent scripture to support the concept. The denomination's leader gladly read the information and politely responded that the writing was very persuasive and convincing but was the type of writing that would be hard to support as it may cause controversy. I was pleased to be described as a persuasive writer yet not surprised that there would be no support for abstract thoughts that might cause controversy.

The interesting part is that within two years of writing about this, two of the leading denominations' main buildings were struck by severe weather, including the one I sent the writing to. Both denominations reported that this kind of severe weather had never struck the downtown areas where their buildings were. One of them reported that the denomination needed to think of a severe weather plan, as weather patterns have changed. Immediately, one of my favorite weather versus came to mind: "He [God] marches out in the whirlwind [tornado] and the raging storm; dark storm clouds billow like dust under his feet." (Nahum 1:3b)

Needless to say, 2006 through 2011 were very trying years for Pam and me as we were way beyond coming out of the closet and now had writings on some of the following things, to name a few:

1. *What in Heaven and Hell is Happening? A complete book explaining the clashing of a spiritual timeline.*
2. *Is Your Head in the Clouds? The O'Manna Plan.*

3. *Our Great Cloud of Witnesses: Close Encounters of the Heavenly Kind.*
4. *The Great Clergy Fall Out.*
5. *Severe weather is only responding to the voice of God.*
6. *What does God's Voice Sound like right before His Return; Rushing Water.*
7. *All Jonah's Overboard—Are you Ready for the tidal wave?*
8. *Slum Dog Christian-heirs.*
9. *And God Chose Dreams: A book documenting the reality that the majority of doctrinal beliefs were defined and explained within dreams and visions, yet the church ignores dreams and visions.*
10. *God is managing our human delusion.*
11. *Spiritual Light Deprivation.*
12. *The Pearl Within: The redemptive nature of reflection.*
13. *God loves the underdog—are you ready for the next phenomenal move of God.*
14. *Reconnecting with your past to gain your future.*

These are just a few of the "out of the normal" messages that are all available for viewing at http://www.focusonheaven.com.

As time progressed and these messages that were slightly ahead of their time become reality, God began turning the tables on us. Suddenly, as each of these messages had been out for public viewing for a few years and people slowly started calling or emailing us with their realities, God whispered in our ears: *Mike and Pam, the facts are now on your side.* Very few humans can experience the feelings that came with this kind of whisper as it was vindicating and sorrowful at the same time. It feels good to be vindicated years after the fact! However, it is still frightful that there can be so much delusion. It is beyond surreal when a person loses his or her reputation among religious groups only to witness the fallout years later and find out that God favored the person who had been asked to leave. As time passed, many calls started arriving to my fourth-generation cell phone with some of the following messages:

+ Mike, how did you know to write the book *What in Heaven*

and Hell is Happening, and include things that had not yet occurred?

- ✦ Mike, there is not a week that goes by now where I do not ask the question and think of your book What in *Heaven and Hell is Happening,* please write a sequel.
- ✦ Mike, as soon as I read the article on God is managing our delusion, I realized the delusion I was living in through an exact experience like you described.

Yes, Pam and I ran the risk of feeling self-justified, vindicated in a self-righteous manner, and even gloating over being correct on things. However, these risks never became reality because even as we were writing many of the things and being criticized, I would say, "I hope I'm wrong." What I could sense and feel while writing was the exact alignment of God's Word coming to pass over time and the accuracy of God's Word. God was spot-on when He stated in Matthew 5:18, "Not one crossing of a 't' or dotting of an 'i' will go unfilled before the world passes away." Pam and I were only crossing the t's and dotting the i's before God's entire Word comes to pass before this world as we know it passes away. The whisper I heard began to be refined to, *Mike and Pam, the facts are on God's side.* We were only instruments in the great orchestra of the kingdom that was helping show that God's Word is factual and living out as we live in the twenty-first century.

> I tell you the truth, until heaven and earth disappear, not the smallest letter, not the least stroke of a pen, will by any means disappear from the Law until everything is accomplished. (Matthew 5:18)

As God began clarifying the whisper in our ear, He started showing us the reality of heaven and the kingdom in a fresh way. It was in 2011 that we realized a precious reward for us was to write about the pleasures and view of heaven and the reality that people who are willing will begin to see into the heavenly realms. However, along with this came the caution that Jesus gave Nicodemus in John 3:12: "We have told you earthly things, and you would not believe, how then will you believe if we tell you heavenly things?"

In the Old Testament (1 Kings 19:12) God's stated that He speaks to us in a still, small voice or whisper. God's whisper to me again was, *Mike, Many those who did not believe the many earthly things you and others have spoken about will not believe the heavenly things, but don't worry. The facts are on My side through My Word.*

Summary

For many years God has been sifting through humanity, churches, and religions to identify the difference between people who love Him and those who are trying to prove that God loves them. God was sifting Nicodemus in that he sent His Son, proving that He already loved humanity and Nicodemus, and then wanted to see if Nicodemus loved Him.

This is the context of 2 Corinthians 2:9–10 as it states very clearly that God reveals, shows, and gives great things that are way beyond earthly understanding to those who love God:

> However, as it is written: "No eye has seen, no ear has heard, no mind has conceived what God has prepared for those who love him" but God has revealed it to us by his Spirit. The Spirit searches all things, even the deep things of God.

This does not mean we are not saved if we do not see all the things of heaven. God loves all humanity, has saved all humanity, gives eternal life in heaven to those who believe in His Son, Jesus, and finally opens heaven's doors on this earth for those of us who have openly lived as if we loved God versus those of us who just want God to love them. After God's act of love of giving us everything through His Son, He no longer needs to prove He loves us. Rather, He wants to know we love Him so we can be shown the things He has graciously and lovingly prepared for us.

CHAPTER 4

WHEN MY STORY REFLECTS HIS STORY

Because of the tender mercy of our God, by which the rising sun will come to us from heaven to shine on those living in darkness and in the shadow of death, to guide our feet into the path of peace.

—Luke 1:78–79

Imagine who you could be if you heard and saw your truest reflection through a filter of purity and perfection. This filter is exactly what God's light creates through His Son Jesus. And in this filter, our life story is seen in a reflective manner that brings God pleasure.

—Michael L. Mathews

It always amazes me how many people dislike seeing themselves on videos, view themselves in photos, or listen to themselves talk on audio segments. The reason many people do not like seeing their reflection is that they have to see or hear themselves for who they really are. On the one hand, many people can pretend they are really someone else, but when confronted with their images or voices they see their true reflections. On the other hand, others feel their lives are so fragmented, broken, or abnormal that viewing or hearing themselves would bring too much pain. The reflection of who we perceive ourselves to be as physical beings or who we perceive ourselves to be as voices are less important than the reflections of who we are as people living through space and time. God and humanity are less interested in who we reflect in the beauty of our complexions or voices than who we reflect through our lives' actions. God has allowed us to reflect our truest value, beauty, and potential in a story format versus a photo. God collects our life stories and allows us to show and reflect a more comprehensive view of Himself through us.

In 2010, my father told me he wanted to donate some money to a nonprofit such as a missionary or a mission that helps needy people. I asked him to consider taking some of his donation and writing a life testimony that would reflect God's beauty through a part of his life. After a few weeks of considering my offer, he stated that he wanted to tell a life story and asked if I could help. I was glad to help, as this is one of my favorite things to do. I perform a greater function than a camera or video recorder when I help people capture moments in their lives and tell reflective stories that help other people.

Within a few days my dad narrowed his story down to "The day I saved my father, and the day my father saved me." Within a few weeks he had the article published in the local paper in his hometown where he had been a teenager in the 1950s. In his life story he asked people to understand what had taken place during the last sixty years of his life that had created a new reflection, one that was different than the reflection he had as a younger man leading a shattered life. Within days he received numerous emails and calls thanking him for such a powerful life story about who he was and who he had become. That one story reconnected him to numerous people he had lost touch with over the years, but more important, the story reflected how God uses people and how people use God to reflect truthful stories as their lives unfold. When he was sixteen, my dad saved his earthly father's life in a serious accident, and years later God reflected that experience as God saved my dad's life. My dad was able to tell a true story of a life reflection. The wonderful story is at the end of this chapter.

The Communication Style of Story Telling

One of the greatest communication methods throughout history has been telling a good story. Jesus was gifted at telling stories and parables and making them a metaphor of what the kingdom of God and heaven is like. Humanity loves a good story! For this reason billions of books have been sold that tell stories of romance, sports, people, and of course the number-one book ever sold, the Bible, which conveys thousands of stories that together reflect the ultimate story of Jesus Christ.

Another example is when Steve Jobs passed away in October 2011. Within weeks his biography came out and sold millions of copies because readers wanted to read about the "storied" life of Steve Jobs.

The power of the story in human life is the very reason why Satan desires to fragment our lives. Every time our lives become fragmented through divorces, anger, bitterness, finances, strife, loneliness, sickness, and other circumstances, our ability to tell our full story is thwarted, damaged, and derailed.

Heaven 3.0 and this chapter are intended to get every reader excited about the image of their personal stories, family stories, and life stories to do everything they can to pull their life stories back together. If your life has been fragmented or broken, you are in for a treat if you are willing to look at your true reflection, which will display the image of who you were created to become.

The Foundation of the Human Life Story

God is clear in the beginning of the Bible that He was willing to create mankind in His image: "Let us create man in our own image, after our likeness" (Genesis 1:26). God's command means that each of us is designed to live a life that reflects the image of God. We do not have to strive to become His image because we were already created in His image. It is through our own actions that we fragment this perfect image. The fact that we were created in God's image never changes and is constant, but when we allow ourselves or others to inflict us with fragmented views, we become separated from that perfect image.

The more fragmented our lives become, the more our image of God within starts to fade and become unclear. When people become broken fragments, they begin masking their stories and begin to hide how they perceive the perfect image (story) of who they were designed to be. The process of fragmenting our lives is top priority for Satan, who knows our stories must be limited and fragmented to prevent us from reflecting our beauty. The reason he knows our stories must be limited is the fact that Revelation 12:10–12 clearly explains that our testimonies and the blood of the Lamb, Jesus, are the only two things that prevent Satan from being victorious over us.

God knows that humanity loves complete stories and that a complete story is able to reflect God's story, as He represents perfection. Every time I tell a great story of what God has done in my life, I am going back to Genesis and stating that I have been created in God's image, so I am reflecting God's story. The image of God within me is the truest form of a testimony or witness that I was created in God's image and that I am on the pathway to heaven!

Satan does all he can do to prevent a person's story from bringing a reflection of God's glory into the world, so he has mastered the art of breaking up our stories. The more fragmented our stories become, the less likely we are to see the reflection of God shine through us. If we were created in the image of God, we are a mirror of Him. The mirror of God can be seen in its completeness when our life stories are in the process of being complete.

Sweetness—The Walter Payton Effect

As people's life stories unfold, they start seeing God's image, and when they see God's image through their lives they become more confident, bold, and assured with their stories. Unfortunately, many people let broken elements in their lives destroy their full stories, causing them to start minimizing God's glory and image through them. My advice to people has and always will be to stop letting circumstances rule our lives. If we are called to rule and reign with Christ, then we need to practice ruling and reigning over circumstances, emotions, and disappointments. Whenever we allow these things to rule over us, the enemy is on the pathway to fragmenting our stories that were meant to be told.

When the great running back Walter Payton played football for the Chicago Bears, he was asked how he had remained injury free and acted as if he were never in pain in spite of the inflictions his body endured each game. He said, "I never give the defense the belief or satisfaction that one of their tackles hurt me because as soon as I do they will see a weakness that will be exploited, and before long I will be injured." In this way he was able to illustrate a life story of greatness on the football field. For this very reason Walter Payton's nickname became "Sweetness." He played, ran, and moved as if he were in charge of the entire football field despite the fact that the defense was out to harm him.

Each of us must realize that God designed us to have the sweetness of His image displayed in and through us even though we sense there are so many things that are against us. This image must be lived and told as witness to God's greatness. This style of living puts Satan in his place while elevating God to His rightful position, which is to be a beautiful reflection in and through us.

When My Life Story Reflects His Story

We must learn to null-and-void the tackles, defenses, and losses of life so they do not interfere with the unfolding of our perfected life stories, which should be continually unfolding in partnership with God. God's story displayed in and through me becomes my main story, which brings credit to His story. God's reflection can be seen in me, and my reflection can be seen in Him. This all brings the fullest story back to how God created me: in His image and likeness. God's ultimate plan for this imagery can be seen through His Son, Jesus Christ. God states that Christ is to be glorified in and through us.

God knew Satan was having a field day in the lives of people by putting doubt, confusion, and brokenness into their paths to prevent them from telling complete and full stories. For this reason God simplified the process of bringing back the image of His creation through humanity by allowing us to accept Jesus into our hearts. Upon that sincere acceptance and confession (Romans 10:9–10), Christ comes into us and quickly allows the image of who God is as well as who we are to reflect (shine) to the world.

Christ in us becomes glorified and reflects the two-way reflection of both God and man. This is why Jesus is called the only intercessor and given the title as the only name under heaven whereby we can be saved. No one else has the ability to clearly reflect the intended image of God and man in order that God's will can be done on earth as it is in heaven. When I allow Christ to be glorified in me, I allow my story to tell God's story, and our perfected image begins to be seen and told through His story and my story combined. The concept I am sharing with you allows us to see why the only prayer given to us by Christ included this aspect of reflection. "Thy Kingdom come, Thy will be done on earth as it is in heaven." God's desire is for us to reflect His image and creation on earth as it has been designed for us in heaven. As history continues to unfold, humanity will start seeing a variety of reflections, pure images that were created and designed by God for humanity. God is a God of order, and He will bring all things full circle back to Genesis, where He created us in His image. Below are a few of the scripture passages that shed insight into the reality that God's glory can be received by us, so that we can reflect back His image and glory.

> We pray this so that the name of our Lord Jesus may be glorified in you, and you in him, according to the grace of our God and the Lord Jesus Christ. — 2 Thessalonians 1:12

Encouraging, comforting and urging you to live lives worthy of God, who calls you into his kingdom and glory. — 1 Thessalonians 2:12

For God, who said, "Let light shine out of darkness," made his light shine in our hearts to give us the light of the knowledge of the glory of God in the face of Christ. — 2 Corinthians 4:6

On the day he comes to be glorified in his holy people and to be marveled at among all those who have believed. This includes you, because you believed our testimony to you. — 2 Thessalonians 1:10

All I have is yours, and all you have is mine. And glory has come to me through them. — John 17:10

Now if we are children, then we are heirs--heirs of God and co-heirs with Christ, if indeed we share in his sufferings in order that we may also share in his glory. I consider that our present sufferings are not worth comparing with the glory that will be revealed in us. — Romans 8:17-18

I pray also that the eyes of your heart may be enlightened in order that you may know the hope to which he has called you, the riches of his glorious inheritance in the saints, — Ephesians 1:18

Our Life Song

The world can smell through people who claim sweetness, greatness, and the kingdom of God and see us live and pray as if we were beggars or complainers in the kingdom. People are and will always be drawn to the story of Christ as they see it reflected in the Bible, a church, a dream, or their life stories. We have lived in an era that has heard and embraced the untrue story of Humpty Dumpty, which clearly reflects the story of brokenness and despair. Consider the main message in Humpty Dumpty: "All the king's horses and all the king's men couldn't put Humpty back together again." A minimum of four generations have heard this story of brokenness, and it is time for these four generations to reverse this broken curse and reflect a story of completeness by letting our glory reflect toward the kingdom as Christ becomes glorified through our complete stories.

If your life story is broken and your perfected story has become fragmented, you will not be able to see your beauty and image as God sees it. In these cases the enemy has temporarily fulfilled God's Word in your life: "The thief comes not but to kill, steal, and destroy" (John 10:10). It is time for you to pull a Walter Payton and jump back up on the playing field of life and start scoring for the kingdom of God with your complete life story, which is the second half of John 10:10: "But I am come that you might have life and life more abundantly."

Our prayer and concern for the world today has little to do with politics, finances, joblessness, etc. Rather, it is the untold story of broken lives that have inhibited the greatest reflection, God on earth as He is seen in heaven. Every broken life is a candle that went dim on earth, and the enemy gloats over another life story that may not be told to reflect God's story. We desire and pray for you to pick up the pieces of your life and allow Christ in to redeem any brokenness. This will allow you to begin to recollect and unfold the story that God always intended for you. Step back in the recesses of your mind and allow God to erase the failures, missteps, and brokenness and redeem it for a quick pathway to the very person He created you to become.

Many people may weep their way through this chapter as they sense how applicable the fragmentation and brokenness I described reflects their lives more than the glory of God does. May I encourage you to realize that any weeping is God's cleansing process that will allow you to embrace by faith His ability to heal, cleanse, and restore your life in order that more of His story can be told through your story. Your weeping is merely an act of faith stating, "I believe that God created me in His image, has a design for my life, and allows me to redeem my missed steps through Christ. This act of confession and faith allows me to begin to reflect His Story through My new future story" (Romans 10:9–10).

A Testimony of Reflection: Living Proof

Early in this chapter I shared the story of my father telling a wonderful story of his life that allowed God and him to reflect the power of life. The story is evidence of what the Bible states and this chapter on reflecting a story of Christ in you. A former childhood friend of my father who read the story tracked down my father and told him that his life story was the best form of the Gospel he had ever read. I was blessed to meet this man a few months later, and he stated that he prints this story and gives it to everyone he meets that needs to hear a story of the reflective power of God:

The Day I Saved my Father ...
and the Day My Father Saved Me!

By Norman Mathews

Hello, my name is Norman Mathews from Eau Claire, Wisconsin. As a young man I was raised in the Daggett, Michigan, area. My parents were Dale and Doris Mathews. I later returned to the area during 1963—1969 as a floundering alcoholic. Like many people from the area back in the 1950s, we worked in the woods, cutting and skidding poplar to sell. When I was fourteen years old, I had one of the strangest ordeals of my life. Little did I know that this same type of supernatural experience would occur to me in a different way later on in life!

Let me tell you about the first experience. I was fourteen years of age and working with my father, Dale Mathews, in the woods. My father was skidding wood, and the dray got caught on a stump, causing the tractor to tip over. When my father landed head first into a tree, his head was split wide open and blood was gushing out. Immediately my senses and surroundings turned into a combination of both a slow motion and fast motion experience. On one hand, everything appeared in slow motion, and I could sense everything around me in a way that I had never experienced before. On the other hand, everything appeared in fast motion where time sped up in an incredible manner. What happened in those few seconds would be an experience I will never forget.

I immediately cradled my father in my arms and ran down the hill and through the swamp a half mile to our house all within what appeared to be less than a second in time. It was that slow-motion and fast-motion experience that made everything appear as if only one second in time had passed between the incident and running the half mile home. When I got home, my mother and I drove him to Dr. Heidenreich's office, where his head was stitched up. Dr. Heidenreich stated that if we would not have gotten him there this quickly he would have bled to death.

In this experience it was clear that my action saved my father's life, but I did not understand what had taken place. I described the experience to Dr. Heidenreich, and he stated that it was an "adrenaline" rush that allowed this experience to occur.

For years I had forgotten about the feeling that I experienced that day. However, this past year I heard someone describe an experience called a "quickening" experience. A quickening experience is when the presence of the Holy Spirit "quickens" a person and their surroundings, and suddenly the awareness of time feels as if it is nonexistent, or when slow motion and fast motion are occurring at the same time. This type of experience also occurred when Jesus Christ died on the cross. If you look in Matthew 27:45–56, you will find that when Jesus died, the entire surroundings in time changed. The Bible states that it became dark for three hours, there was an earthquake, and some dead people rose from their graves and walked into Jerusalem. Within a split second of time, things were potentially fast-motion, slow-motion, and even reversed insomuch that people who were dead were now alive again. This is not hard to fathom when you consider that Jesus was being quickened from this earthly life to His eternal home. During that quickening moment heaven and earth were shaken. Romans 8:11 shares that this quickening experience does happen to people by saying "But if the Spirit of him that raised up Jesus from the dead dwell in you, he that raised up Christ from the dead shall also quicken your mortal bodies by his Spirit that dwelleth in you."

This awareness of the power of the Holy Spirit brings me to my second supernatural experience, which is a more ongoing and progressive experience that has occurred over a thirty-year period of time. Through Christ's love I have been eternally saved, been healed of colon cancer, delivered through triple bypass surgery, and spared on numerous other occasions.

For twenty-five years I was a hopeless alcoholic and a very angry person like many other people in the Wisconsin and Upper Peninsula area. Yes, I worked hard, raised my seven children, and have been married for fifty-three years, but deep within I was an eternally dead man who was pushing his way through life. At this juncture in my life I can now see a critical comparison: just as my father back in the woods was a dead man without my "quickening experience," I was also a dead man without a "quickening experience" occurring in my life. The quickening experience with my father allowed me to redeem enough time to get him to the doctor's office before he bled to death, and the quickening experience from my heavenly Father (God) through the Holy Spirit allowed me to redeem the lost years of time.

Possibly you are like I was: you drink, get angry, are bitter, and have no eternal hope. If this is you, this is the reason for this story. As my brother-in-law Jimmy LaCass told me one day, "Norman, if a drunk like you can quit drinking, anyone can quit drinking." In the most basic sense he was right, but he did not know the secret of my changed life. My life changed through my heavenly Father saving me by accepting the transforming power of His son Jesus Christ. Christ shined his light into my life, which allowed me to see that Jesus Christ died for a mean alcoholic like me. His 'light' was powerful and transforming and quickened my life from its dead nature. My life was quickened, and just as I saved my father's life, my heavenly Father saved my life. In both cases the quickening experience redeemed the time that was lost. I had lost many years to the power of alcohol, and God wanted to redeem these lost years. I can now thank God for the redemptive process.

If you or someone you know is under the power of some ungodly influence, I would like you to know that you can experience this same quickening (redeeming) in your life. All you have to do is accept Jesus into your heart using the three simple steps stated below.

At this point in my story I would like to extend an offer of forgiveness to anyone who I have wronged in my past. I have learned that all healings and blessings begin on our knees, where God can meet us and give us answer to all our prayers. If you have had any similar experiences like I did, I would love to hear from you.

The ABCs of Salvation: To know God and be ready for heaven and redeem your lost years follow these simple steps:

A. Admit you are a sinner.

"There is no one righteous, not even one … for all have sinned and fall short of the glory of God" (Romans 3:10,23; also see Romans 5:8; 6:23). Ask God's forgiveness. "Everyone who calls on the name of the Lord will be saved" (Romans 10:13).

B. Believe in Jesus.

Put your trust in Him as your only hope of salvation. "For God so loved the world that he gave his one and only Son, that whoever believes in him shall not perish but have eternal life" (John 3:16; also see John 14:6). Become a child of God by receiving Christ. "To all who receive him, to those who believed in his name, he gave the right to become children of God" (John 1:12; also see Revelation 3:20).

C. Confess that Jesus is your Lord.

"That if you confess with your mouth, 'Jesus is Lord,' and believe in your heart that God raised him from the dead, you will be saved" (Romans 10:9).

CHAPTER 5

WATER AND BLOOD HAVE LIFE, MEMORY, AND REFLECTION

As in water the face is reflected as a face, so a person's heart reflects the person.

—Proverbs 27:19

This is the one who came by water and blood—Jesus Christ. He did not come by water only, but by water and blood. And it is the Spirit who testifies, because the Spirit is the truth. For there are three that testify: the Spirit, the water and the blood; and the three are in agreement.

—1 John 5:6–8

As we discuss the higher elements of being able to see heaven in a fresh, new, and revealing way, you may be asking: What has changed in order to start seeing heavenly things on a more frequent basis? How does the process of seeing into the supernatural or heavenly actually occur?

In this chapter we will look at the possible means that all refection takes place in order to be more cognizant and aware of the increase in visions, dreams, miracles, and heavenly observations. We could end this chapter by stating that it is occurring simply because God stated it would happen (Acts 2:17–21), but what may help a lot of people is to start understanding the process God may use for people to receive the fullness of His blessings in a more frequent and natural manner.

First Things First

Before diving into the explanation, it is fitting to first and foremost give God credit for the increase in dreams, visions, and heavenly observations. In Acts 2:17–19 God speaks through the apostle Peter and tells the world that in the last days there will be a sequential and increased manner of the supernatural, miraculous, and natural phenomena in the last days. As you read Acts 2:17–19 please note the following aspects:

1. There will be an increase in dreams, visions, and prophecies among old and young people.
2. Sons and daughters (young people) will begin to prophesy.
3. Servants will begin to prophesy (this means anyone and everyone).
4. There will be natural signs and wonders in the heavens.

In the last days, God says, I will pour out my Spirit on all people. Your sons and daughters will prophesy, your young men will see visions, your old men will dream dreams. Even on my servants, both men and women, I will pour out my Spirit in those days, and they will prophesy. I will show wonders in the heaven above and signs on the earth below, blood and fire and billows of smoke. (Acts 2:17–19)

God clearly states the facts that as the last of days of this world progress, we will naturally start seeing more of the miraculous through dreams, visions, and signs in the heavens.

Reflection of Reality

God's Word has always been accurate, and as time moves forward it is proving itself through the manifestations of individuals around the world. One example is the hundreds of news reports that millions of people in the Middle East have experienced vivid dreams of revelations that allowed them to change their viewpoint of religion, God, and the kingdom of God. These reports have come from all types of reporters, magazines, and newspapers between 2008 and 2012.

The method by which God is allowing people to experience, visualize, and touch the realms of heaven is through reflection, which includes the reflection of heaven and earth, the reflection of our past, and the reflection of our future. How this reflection is happening is through the creation of water and light. This may sound way too simple, but once you step back and realize that God states that He is Light and that Christ came through water and blood, it begins to make perfect sense.

> This is the message we have heard from him and declare to you: God is light; in him there is no darkness at all. (1 John 1:5)

> This is the one who came by water and blood—Jesus Christ. He did not come by water only, but by water and blood. And it is the Spirit who testifies, because the Spirit is the truth. (1 John 5:6)

All reflection and truth comes from light, and water is the only substance that reflects full color when light shines upon it. Jesus came by water and blood to reflect the love of God to the world, and that water was left to represent the full reflection of God. Christ came by water and blood, and when He was crucified, both water and blood came from His side. More interesting is that a molecule of water never disappears from earth; it just travels the hydrocycle. For this reason God states that there are three things that testify on earth: the Spirit, water, and blood.

- Instead, one of the soldiers pierced Jesus' side with a spear, bringing a sudden flow of blood and water. (John 19:34)

- And there are three that bear witness in earth, the Spirit, and the water, and the blood: and these three agree in one. (1 John 5:7–8 KJV)

Imagine if we could start seeing heavenly and hidden things by identifying the reflective capabilities given to us. This capability would allow us to piece together things from our past, present, and future. It would allow us to literally fulfill some of the promises of God, such as whatever we bind on earth will be bound in heaven, and whatever we loose on earth will be loosed in heaven (Matthew 16:19).

If we could see human and heavenly reflections in a vivid manner, suddenly the issues of religions, denominations, laws, and doctrinal differences would start to vanish because the truth can be seen in full reflection, whereas only partial truth can be found in the shadows of reflection. Most religious belief systems are formed in the shadows of the real truth. A shadow or copy of the real truth can make people believe that they are really doing the right thing even though it is only a figure, copy, or shadow of the full truth. The partial truth or "shadow of the truth" concept is exactly what the Apostle Paul states about the church and Christ in Hebrews 9:24:

> For Christ did not enter a man-made sanctuary that was only a copy of the true one; he entered heaven itself, now to appear for us in God's presence. (Hebrews 9:24)

Jesus Himself did not come through what we know as church buildings, synagogues, temples, or basilicas because these buildings made by human hands represent only a human understanding of God. They are mere shadows, copies, or figures of the real truth that cause so many differences of opinion. However, heaven itself represents the full truth of who we are in Christ.

The reflection of the full truth comes only from God through Christ, who sits on the right hand of God the Father in heaven. How this happens is through the power of blood and water reflected by God's Light. This concept is very enlightening as it helps us start seeing how simple the truth really is! Remember, Christ came by "water and blood" and left "water and blood" when he died. And with water's hydrocycle, the blood and water He left never disappear, so they never lose their powers. Water is the only substance in heaven and earth that has the ability to reflect full color and represent the truth of how something truly appears. Whenever a source of light casts a shadow over water, the water displays full-color reflection. If you were in a downtown city area surrounded by a waterfront and the sunrise or moon cast a shadow of the city skyline on that water, the skyline would appear in full color on top of the water. The ability of water to cast full-color reflections is the primary reason the majority of heaven and earth are filled with water. God created approximately 70 percent of heaven and earth with water, which will be discussed momentarily.

What is important to note is the aspects of water that make heaven and earth reflect each other. The three key aspects of God's design, which are critical to comprehend in reference to water, are 1.) Creation was designed with two large bodies of water that reflect each other. One body of water is in heaven, and the other is on earth. 2.) Christ came by water and blood, and that water and blood reflect toward heaven what is happening on earth. 3.) Many of the miracles performed included water. In fact, thirty-seven miracles recorded in scripture involved water. The reason water was included was due to God's understanding of the universal laws of water. These three aspects are described in scripture and help us believe and see the aspects of the full kingdom of God, which includes heaven and earth. Let's take a snapshot view of water from physical and spiritual perspectives.

Physical Attributes of Water

+ Water covers 70 percent of earth.
+ Human bodies are made up of 60 to 70 percent water.
+ The human brain is made up of over 70 percent water.
+ Water constitutes 83 percent of our blood.
+ Water is the only substance on earth that exists and can be transformed into three forms: liquid, solid, and gas.

- Water changes forms but never disappears. One molecule of water travels earth for over 10 billion years. This hydrocycle and fact can be read in detail at http://earthobservatory.nasa.gov/Features/Water/water_2.php
- Water is the most cohesive among nonmetallic liquids, meaning things adhere to water molecules.
- Water is one of the only liquids that transports through osmosis, by traveling in and out of cell membranes. For example, water can travel through the membranes of trees to reach the center of the tree and the top of the tree.
- Sound travels through water four and a half times faster and much louder than through air.
- The Moon's gravitational pull causes water to change direction and to cause high tides and low tides.
- Water is one of the only substances that naturally have a multidimensional flow.
- Water is one of the "true" reflectors of full color and image.
- Water is one of the greatest conduits of light.
- Water is one of the greatest conduits of electricity.
- When a physician wants to do an ultrasound, the patient must drink large amounts of water to allow the ultrasound waves to reflect the images off the water in the body.
- Science has recently found that water retains memory. Sounds strange, but this has resurfaced as a new finding by science that helps explains some of the capabilities of water. Even though there is debate by scientists, it would explain many of the miracles that have taken place with water.
- Water in outer space is 1.4 trillion times more than the water on earth.
  - Two teams of astronomers have discovered the largest and farthest reservoir of water ever detected in the universe. The water, equivalent to 140 trillion times all the water in the world's ocean, surrounds a huge, feeding black hole, called a quasar, more than 12 billion light years away.
  - "The environment around this quasar is very unique in that it's producing this huge mass of water," said

Matt Bradford, a scientist at NASA's Jet Propulsion Laboratory in Pasadena, California. "It's another demonstration that water is pervasive throughout the universe, even at the very earliest times." Bradford leads one of the teams that made the discovery. His team's research is partially funded by NASA and appears in the Astrophysical Journal Letters.

Spiritual Aspects of Water

+ The entire creation was water before the earth was formed.
  ▶ "Now the earth was formless and empty, darkness was over the surface of the deep, and the Spirit of God was hovering over the waters." (Genesis 1:2).
+ There are two expanses of water, one in heaven and one on earth.
  ▶ And God said, "Let there be an expanse between the waters to separate water from water. So God made the expanse and separated the water under the expanse from the water above it. And it was so. God called the expanse 'sky,'" (Genesis 1:6–8)
+ People are baptized in water for a symbol of purification (1 Peter 3:21).
  ▶ God cleansed the earth in Noah's day with water through the forty-day flood. This also proved the expanse of water that was in heaven.
  ▶ "In the six hundredth year of Noah's life, in the second month, the seventeenth day of the month, the same day were all the fountains of the great deep broken up, and the windows of heaven were opened. And the rain was upon the earth forty days and forty nights." (Genesis 7:11–12)
+ Jesus's first miracle was turning water into wine.
+ Jesus used water to wash the disciples' feet.
+ When Jesus's side was pierced by the Roman soldiers, water, not just blood, came out.
+ Jesus is referred to as the living water of life (John 4:14).
+ Christ came by water and blood (1 John 5:6).

- ✦ Miracles of water are documented thirty-seven times.
- ✦ Water expressed as the "reflective nature of church, marriage, and self" (Ephesians 5).
- ✦ Jesus's voice sounds like "rushing water" before His return (Revelation 1:15).

Water is the conduit to how life flows, things are cleansed, and how true-color reflection occurs, so it should make sense why God states that Jesus came by water and blood and why He left water and blood behind. Even if the water and blood that Christ left behind during his death was even one molecule, it continues to circulate the earth through water's hydrocycle. Water and blood are how we can see our reflection in Christ and be saved from the false images and shadows that have cluttered our minds. This over simplistic view is validated in Jesus's simple message to Nicodemus:

> I tell you the solemn truth unless a man be born of the water and spirit he cannot enter the Kingdom of God. (John 3:5)

Unless we are born of water and the Spirit via the water and blood of Jesus, we cannot enter the kingdom of God. Water, blood, and Spirit are the three things as we stated from 1 John 5:7 that are in agreement and testify of things on earth. Many scholars explain being born of water as our first natural birth. More probable is the simple reality that Jesus was conveying that until we are born of the one who came by water and blood and the Spirit, we cannot enter the kingdom. Getting even more precise would be a statement from Jesus much like, "Until you are willing to believe that I am in you and you are in me, you cannot enter the kingdom of God." Refining it even further, Jesus would be saying, "Until you have the faith to see your reflection in me and my reflection in you, you cannot enter the kingdom of God."

Jesus desires us all to know we can see our original birth through Jesus who came by way of water and blood. We can see this birth by seeing that we were originally created in the image of God. If we see ourselves in Christ and He sees himself in us, we can see the full and true reflection of who we were from the beginning, which was created in God's image. This may be a new thought for many people reading this simple message, but it is the reality of humanity being created in God's image from the beginning. Colossians 1:27 explains that this is so simple it has been a mystery that God had been waiting to show through His son, Jesus. Read Colossians 1:27 below and see if you are capable of processing the simple faith that allows you to see your reflection in Christ and therefore His reflection in you! When you can have this faith and allow your imagination or true reflection to be seen, you will start revealing God's glory.

- To them God has chosen to make known among the Gentiles the glorious riches of this mystery, which is Christ in you, the hope of glory. (Colossians 1:27)

- This mystery has been kept in the dark for a long time, but now it's out in the open. God wanted everyone, not just Jews, to know this rich and glorious secret inside and out, regardless of their background, regardless of their religious standing. The mystery in a nutshell is just this: Christ is in you, so therefore you can look forward to sharing in God's glory. It's that simple. (Colossians 1:26–27 MSG)

God's desire has always been to have His glory reflected and shine through His people. God adds a helpful passage of scripture that allows us to realize that when we die to our earthly ways and earthly birth we make a decision to be hidden with Christ. Christ becomes our shield, protector, and intercessor who blocks out our former images of guilt, pride, shame, sin, and dysfunction.

For you have died and your life is hidden with Christ in God. (Colossians 3:3)

Think about the significance of this simple truth of God's light reflecting upon His water and blood, His son, Jesus, that allows you to see and experience the perfect image and plan for you personally. This is the message that God gave to humanity. Unfortunately it is so simple that people overlook the simplicity of it all.

Reflections from a Different Angle

God desires us to reverse the earthly or fleshly way we process life and see into the realm of heavenly possibilities, which is through Him. As human beings we have a tendency to try to not be like our earthly parents or see ourselves through our children. Many adults get frustrated when they realize they see the same behaviors, attributes, personalities, and even images in their children that are in themselves. On the other hand, children work for years trying to run from the fact that they do not want to grow up to be like their parents, only to find out in the end that they are much like them from the earthly perspective.

God knows this trait in humans and therefore gives each of us the permission, opportunity, and blessing to look far beyond earthly or fleshly parents and imagine our reflection from a heavenly perspective. This image is our original birth, in God's image. Think about this as you read the conversation between Jesus and Nicodemus again:

> Nicodemus replied, "How can these things be?" Jesus answered, "Are you the teacher of Israel and yet you don't understand these things? I tell you the solemn truth, we speak about what we know and testify about what we have seen, but you people do not accept our testimony. If I have told you people about earthly things and you don't believe, how will you believe if I tell you about heavenly things?" (John 3:9–12)

God's light and ability to reflect heaven and earth are simple concepts, yet may people make them more complicated than they need be. Considering that water reflects and there are bodies of water in heaven and earth, it is easy to see why Jesus stated that we should pray the Lord's Prayer, which includes, "Thy Kingdom come, Thy will be done on earth as it is in heaven" (Matthew 6:10). He also instructs us that we have the keys to the kingdom, that whatever is bound on earth will be bound in heaven, and that whatever we loose on earth will be loosed in heaven (Matthew 16:19).

As a simple illustration I could make a statement such as, "Mike, stand in front of the mirror and realize that whatever you do will be also done in the mirror, as it is a complete reflection of your actions." The mirror is my reflection because light shines on me and goes to the mirror. Without light, there is absolutely no reflection of me in the mirror. This same concept taken at the atmospheric level between heaven and earth can be said of God. God is light, and in Him there is no darkness at all. God's light in every aspect of life and existence allows the reflection of His work to be seen between heaven and earth:

> This is the message we have heard from him and declare to you:
> God is light; in him there is no darkness at all. (1 John 1:5)

God's design was to send Jesus by water and blood so His fullest light could reflect on the being and purpose of His Son. This light and reflection allows us to come out of the shadow and into full light and reflection, which in turn allows us to see our original image of being created in God.

> Leaving Nazareth, he [Jesus] went and lived in Capernaum, which was by the lake in the area of Zebulun and Naphtali to fulfill what was said through the prophet Isaiah: "Land of Zebulun and land of Naphtali, the way to the sea, along the Jordan, Galilee of the Gentiles—the people living in darkness have seen a great light; on those living in the land of the shadow of death a light has dawned. (Matthew 4:13–15)

> But we all, with unveiled face, beholding as in a mirror the glory of the Lord, are being transformed into the same image from glory to glory, just as from the Lord, the Spirit. (2 Corinthians 3:18 NASB)

Blood and Water Are Powerful Conduits in Everyday Life

Without blood there is no life, and without water, life cannot be sustained. In the cycle of life, blood is the one element that keeps breath going in the physical sense. The Bible re-emphasizes the fact that life is in the blood. As soon as blood stops pumping and processing in any body, it dies. Water is required to keep the blood pumping and makes up 83 percent of the blood in the body. Water is the miracle aspect of all life and lives in every realm of nature and every creature. Because water is the only substance on earth that has three forms, its life cycle is unique and transparent as it takes on three different forms (gas, solid, and liquid). The water cycle for one single water molecule over a hundred-year period includes spending ninety-eight years in the ocean, twenty months as ice, about two weeks in lakes and rivers, and less than a week in the atmosphere. (Keep this in mind as you read my story below). The hydrocycle describes the pilgrimage of water molecules as they make their way from the earth's surface to the atmosphere and back again. This gigantic system, powered by energy from the sun, is a continuous exchange of moisture between the oceans, the atmosphere, and the land.

Water continues to amaze scientists as they continue to find new attributes of water. The most recent finding (circa 2011) is that water has the ability to retain memory. In other words, water molecules can remember former states that they were in as well as display new attributes depending on what they are surrounded and exposed to.

This "water-memory" theory was first proposed by the late French immunologist Dr. Jacques Benveniste in a controversial article published in 1988 in *Nature* magazine as a way of explaining how homeopathy works. Benveniste's theory has continued to be championed by some and disputed by others.

However, some fascinating recent experiments with water "memory" from the Aerospace Institute of the University of Stuttgart in Germany validate the original findings. (A report by the Institute of Aerospace Thermodynamics at the University of Stuttgart in Germany on this topic is at http://odewire.com/170441/scientists-investigate-water-memory.html.)

> "If Benveniste is right, just think what that might mean. More than 70 percent of our planet is covered in water. The human body is made of 60 percent water; the brain, 70 percent; the lungs, nearly 90 percent. Our energies might be traveling out of our brains and bodies and into those of other living beings of all kinds through imprints on this magical substance. The oceans and rivers and rains might be transporting all manner

of information throughout the world. I like to believe that the good doctor was correct—if for no other reason than the phrase "the memory of water" makes my heart leap and spin." **Source:** Odewire, News for Intelligent Optimists; Dec. 8, 2011

Dreams and Water

As science continues to figure out what is happening, God continues to fulfill His promises. Imagine with me the power of water if it has memory and retains information on where it has traveled and what it is exposed to! This capability may start explaining what takes place in the dream life. Have you ever had a vivid dream in which you were traveling in a different space in time? During these types of dreams have you experienced any of the following?

1. You awoke from a dream completely shocked at how real the dream appeared to be?
2. You awoke from a dream and found that the back of your neck was moist or sweating.
3. You awoke from a dream and felt completely exhausted throughout the day.

These experiences are often repeated when we have dreams in which we travel through space and time. Now let's apply the physical, chemical, and spiritual attributes of water to what may be occurring by considering the following:

A. If water has the capacity to go through the membranes of solid trees, surely water can travel in and out of the membranes of our porous bodies even while we sleep.

B. If water is a conduit for electricity and can carry light and sound faster than any other substance, surely water can travel to different spaces in time while we sleep.

C. If light travels at 183,000 miles per second and water mixed with light can be transported, that would mean that water can travel throughout my lifetime in a few seconds. No wonder dreams are but a few seconds long but can travel through different aspects (spaces and times) of my life.

D. If water remembers former states it was in and can be transferred by light, water may leave my body without me really knowing it. It would also be capable of coming back.

E. If my brain is 70 percent water, and water can sense the thoughts and intents of what I am expressing, it would make sense why I dream of things I dwelled on during the day and explain why my hopes can be seen in my dream life.

F. If water can come and go between former states, conditions, and between liquids, solids, and gases, this may explain how water was turned into wine and Jesus walked on water as if it were a solid. At a minimum, Jesus, coming as water and blood, would understand the chemical, physical, and spiritual properties of water.

G. If water can retain where it was before, and I confess with my mouth that the water and blood that Jesus spilled was exactly what God says it was, for my salvation, the salvation experience makes sense in that it literally changes my life. When I truly repent and accept Jesus, suddenly my whole nature changes. That same water that comes from Jesus via heaven does exactly what Jesus said it would: "Create in me rivers of living water" (John 7:38). When I accepted Jesus, my dream live was completely reversed.

Now before you think I'm crazy, let's test your openness. Each of you reading this book can lie in bed with your Smartphone and think it is completely normal to transmit text, data, photos, and even videos across the world through thin air. No one thinks it strange or odd that these signals are being transferred through thin air through electrical signals and impulses that travel in the air at the speed of light (yes even during the evening). The mechanics of this include a transmitter and receiver of the signals, but nonetheless they travel right past your face, into your cell phone, in the atmosphere. Somehow we are able to believe and receive the reality that images can pass through air into hardware devices created by humans but struggle to believe that spiritual signals can be transmitted in the supernatural realm. Considering God is Light and created all things, including the cosmos, hydrogen, oxygen, water, and all the physical, chemical, and spiritual elements to transmit any kind of signal across the airwaves, why is it strange to think that God can transmit vivid reality into any mind that is an open receiver to the things of God?

Our inability to take God at face value and receive heavenly viewings helps explain why the sightings of heavenly things occur more frequently during life-and-death matters than on a regular basis. When people are faced with death-defying circumstances, they are more in tune with the supernatural because suddenly their "reception" of God's transmissions are more in tune with what has always been available. My personal desire is to see more people tune in their reception and act as if God is able 100 percent of the time to communicate rather than just a few times when we are in desperate circumstances. We need to reverse our trust in God so we receive the same amount of communication over the heavenly airwaves as we do signals over the cell waves. Our fullest reflection depends upon reversing our view of God's desire and ability to communicate with us through the means He has available.

One day science will catch up with God and help people intersect the facts that have been recorded in scripture with what is being understood. In the meantime it is the right of every human being to envision the great things God has prepared for all those who love Him (1 Corinthians 2:9–10). We have the pleasure of imagining and receiving the promises that have been proven from God. Human beings dream and often travel places within those dreams through time and space. At times the dreams and visions are in the past, at other times they are in the future, and still other times they occur simultaneously in the present, past, and future. Throughout human history people have been dreaming with often phenomenal results, will you believe. Pam and I have written *And God Chose Dreams*, a book that documents all the dreams and visions recorded in scripture, and it will enlighten you to the reality that God reflected His glory toward people throughout history through dreams.

CHAPTER 6

LIGHT VERSUS LOVE

Arise, shine, for your light has come, and the glory of the LORD rises (shines) upon you.

—Isaiah 60:1

You will never meet your fullest future until God's light transcends your past, present and future to reconnect you to who He always created you to be.

—Michael L. Mathews

The image in Figure 6.1 is a picture of a photo of what meteorologists call a "cloud halo," a ring of light that seems to encircle the sun or moon when veiled by cirrus clouds. This phenomenon is created when cirrus clouds are in a diverse arrangement to reflect and refract the sunlight through the ice crystals in the clouds. The ice crystals in the cirrus clouds serve as prisms that reflect and refract light.

Figure 6.1: Cloud Halo

Figure 6.2 is another example of a halo that represents a complete circle of brilliance produced by the ice crystal prisms in cirrus clouds. The prisms or ice crystals are so connected to each other that it results in a form that represents completeness.

Figure 6.2: Cloud Circle

If the fragments or pieces of your life were connected like these ice crystal prisms, your life would also produce the same form of symmetry and completeness as the cloud halo, and it would include your past, present, and future. If you could imagine that this type of completeness is possible, the only missing ingredient would be the source of light that shines through the crystals of your past, present, and future. This may sound way too simple, yet this is the journey of a complete life and this particular chapter.

In order for this type of journey to make sense, you must understand that God may be much bigger, broader, and more phenomenal that you ever thought possible. Let it be known that God desires, longs, and waits for you to allow this greater aspect of Him to shine in all aspects of your life, including your past, present and future.

Bringing Out the Often-Missed Aspect of God

Modern society has been overexposed to many of the favorable aspects of God that have blinded us to often forgotten key aspects of God, including His aspect of being the light of life, which is described in scripture:

> Praise the LORD, O my soul. O LORD my God, you are very great; you are clothed with splendor and majesty. He wraps himself in light as with a garment; he stretches out the heavens like a tent and lays the beams of his upper chambers on their waters. He makes the clouds his chariot and rides on the wings of the wind." (Psalm 104:1–3)

> When Jesus spoke again to the people, he said, I am the light of the world. Whoever follows me will never walk in darkness, but will have the light of life. (John 8:12)

> While I am in the world, I am the light of the world. (John 9:5)

> I have come into the world as a light, so that no one who believes in me should stay in darkness. (John 12:46)

> This is the message we have heard from him and declare to you:
> God is light; in him, there is no darkness at all. (1 John 1:5)

We all need to appreciate the many attributes of God such as love, mercy, grace, kindness, justice, and so forth, but when we finally see God as light and understand how powerful and transforming light is, we may have an opportunity to allow that light to both reflect and refract upon our lives. When we comprehend this light, we can start seeing God's beauty and how it allows us to reflect our own. When we refuse or unknowingly deny this light, we lose sight of God's true power. Without comprehending this light, searching for the beauty or happiness within us may be a long, wasted journey. This light is not connected to a religion, denomination, belief system, church, group, or tribe; it is unfiltered and freely available to everyone willing to acknowledge and seek it.

The reason many people miss the foundational element of God being light is simply because we all strive for love. Because we search so hard and desperately for love, we tend to cling to people, relationships, spouses, and churches and even believe in the portions of God that make us feel loved. Love is important, but love by itself does not illuminate things or speed things up. In fact, love mixed with passion often blinds people. This explains why people who see only love without light get blindsided fairly frequently in their relationships and religion. We can biblically and appropriately say that without God's Light, His defining attribute, we cannot see love, justice, grace, mercy, kindness, peace, joy, faith, patience, dreams, visions, miracles, or heaven in the purest sense. And without seeing them in their purest sense, we settle for the human version of these attributes.

History has proven that man's versions of these attributes are often manipulated and distorted, which explains why there are hundreds of religions divided on the simple essence of God's grace, mercy, justice, salvation, love, faith, etc. Denominations have not properly reflected the light of life on these attributes simply because they do not put light, God's defining attribute, first!

In heaven, God's Light is so bright that no denomination, theory of love, feeling of acceptance, or belonging can block it. This is why the closer we get a glimpse of heaven the more we see God for who He is! True unity is finally reached because the full and true reflection is seen. In 1 Corinthians 13:10–12 is an attempt to explain it:

> But when perfection comes, the imperfect disappears. When I was a child, I talked like a child, I thought like a child, I reasoned like a child. When I became a man, I put childish ways behind me. Now we see but a poor reflection as in a mirror; then we shall see face to face. Now I know in part; then I shall know fully, even as I am fully known.

Now that we can appreciate that God is Light, let's define some unique characteristics of light. Light's defining characteristics include speed and illumination. Light travels at 186,000 miles per second and illuminates anything in its presence. Light is so fast that it actually reaches its destination at the same time it leaves its starting point. This phenomenal attribute of light is why God references Himself as the great "I AM." Because He is Light, he was at the end at the same time He was at the beginning. Jesus also echoes the same words: "Before I was, I AM." God is therefore able to transcend all time, including my past, present, and future. God's attribute of light means that when my past began, that same light was at the end of my future. It traveled through my past, present, and future simultaneously. It also means that God can and does travel through heaven and earth at the same time. Therefore, we can see that the will of God in heaven is done on earth as well and at the same time.

Hollywood didn't invent time travel; rather, God *is* time travel. He is the great "I AM." Light's speed is the reason God states that one thousand years to humanity is as one day to Him (Psalm 90:4). No wonder God knew me before I was born and knows in advance my choices and ultimate destiny. He as light traveled through my past and destiny before I ever left my mother's womb. On a positive note, it is no wonder he can correct my past and my present and reinvent my future all within a split-second dream, vision, or circumstance. It may also be how He can relate to all my infirmities and temptations; he traveled through them and experienced them before I was born.

Let's compare our human love to God's Light to see the vast contrast between the two and to see why there are so many issues when we strive only for the love side of a relationship. Table 6.1 shows the contrast between love and light.

Attributes of Love	Attributes of Light
Love is more of a feeling than a fact.	Light is more of a fact than a feeling.
Love can be fleeting at times.	Light is constant.
Love can cause us to be blind at times.	Light always exposes blindness/darkness.
When love is pure and true, it feels awesome.	Light is always pure and true.
When love is abused, it hurts or destroys people, feelings, and relationships.	You can never abuse light; it always exposes truth and separates light from darkness.
When love is right, my life improves and goes forward.	Light always improves things and moves things forward.
When love is wrong, my life moves backward.	Light cannot be wrong, and when used it always moves my life forward.
Hatred, bitterness, and envy can squash or minimize human love.	Darkness cannot squash light. There is no conqueror of light.
Variable: can be fast, stagnant, slow, or regressive.	Constant: always fast (travels at 186,000 miles/second).
God did not say, "Let us create love."	God did say, "Let us create light."
God did not say to let your love shine before men so they may see your good works and glorify your father in heaven.	God did say to let your light shine before men, so they see your good works and glorify your father in heaven.
Love lets me like, judge, or dislike someone else.	Light lets me see things for what they really are as it exposes things.

Attributes of Love	Attributes of Light
God did not say "The love of the body is the eye; and if your eye be full of love, your whole body will be full of love."	God did say, "The light of the body is the eye; and if your eye be full of light, your whole body will be full of love." (Matthew 6:22)
Satan does not need to disguise himself as an angel of love because love would cast out fear. "Perfect love casts out all fear." (1 John 4:18)	Satan tries to disguise himself as an angel of light because this is the perfect impersonation of God. Satan tries to reflect himself in our lives. (2 Cor. 11:14)
Medical research did not discover love deprivation disorder.	Medical research did discover light deprivation disorder as part of seasonal affective disorder (SAD).

Table 6.1: The Contrast between Love and Light

By examining Table 6.1 we can rationalize that light is the one constant force that comes from God. His love is also perfect, but humans have a tendency to modify and easily distort His love. The great news is that there is no way humans can distort God's light; they can only ignore it. In the Psalm 23, King David describes the feeling of walking through the valley of the shadow of death yet fearing no evil because a light is shining in his circumstance. He states that there is a shadow, and wherever there is a shadow means that there is also a light shining into the darkness. Without light there can be no shadow.

Imagine the power unleashed when I recognize that God is not just love but light! This revelation of light combined with love was given that we could begin to see things that we never saw before. That light might begin to reflect and refract on the issues of our lives and allow us to finally see the pearls within us that we previously viewed as irritants.

A Personal Example of Light versus Love

Pam likes to share the following example that helped her in our marriage:

> One day this concept of light versus love dawned on me, and I started to search for more meaning in my marriage, my life, and my walk with God. This search allowed me to put the love for Mike in a better perspective. My fear and worry about the limitations of how much we loved each other began to vanish. When I decided to see God's light and the light within Mike, I could see who both God and Mike truly were. The elusive nature of feelings and emotions no longer mattered, whereas they had controlled me in the past. The new reflection of light caused my life, marriage, and relationship with God to skyrocket to a new level, and they continue to grow. Looking back, what I was really saying was that I chose to no longer worry over the elusiveness of love but have a flashlight shined into my life and Mike's life.

> The light of God shines and reveals the reflection of myself in Mike and his reflection into me. We were instantly more compatible, respectful, and true to each other, a feeling we never had when we were fretting if we loved each other. I believe I chose at that moment in my life to let God's light shine and Mike's light shine to the point I found a new respect, new admiration, and new future for my marriage, my relationship, and myself with God. Through this experience or exchange I found that I operated less from emotion and more from facts that light revealed. This should not have surprised me because light exposes facts, while human love expresses emotion.

> Human love had a very strange way of having me always doubt, fear, worry, and at times think evil, condemning, and spiteful thoughts. My experience was a revelation that is explained in Matthew 6:22–23. The light of the body is the eye, and if my eye be single/clear, my whole body will be full of life, but if my eye is evil, my whole body is full of darkness, and oh how great is that darkness. This light that began to shine in me began to

work on my mind rather than just my heart. My newfound light was amazing as things changed and opened up to me like never before. Have you ever noticed that when you buy a different make, model, and color of automobile that suddenly you start noticing how many more people drive the exact same make and model? It now seems as if everyone suddenly has one just like yours. My experience of light is much the same. Once I accepted and allowed God to shine His light upon my life and circumstances, I started to notice things being exposed by His light that had normally been hidden from my view. In addition, my understanding and desire for change sped up. Light fulfilled its purpose in me; it exposed darkness and sped things up.

Now let's take a very personal biblical example that connects the concept that light from God is far superior then the feelings of love. Light has the potential to change circumstances that love by itself cannot. Love from God is phenomenal in many ways.

A Biblical Example of Light versus Love: Acts 9

The religious leader Saul, later named Paul, was a religious leader who initially missed the fact that Jesus Christ was the Messiah, the light that was changing the world. This lack of seeing the light created great confusion for him, and as a religious leader he made a drastic mistake and concurred with his religious peers that Christians must be killed. They were convinced that Christianity was a cult that was working against the organization of religion. Saul/Paul was a zealous religious person who hated the truth of Jesus Christ. One day, when he was on his way to Damascus, an amazing light flashed around him that was so powerful it knocked him off his horse. Immediately Saul knew it was the Lord, who was examining his life at that very moment. Saul knew it was the Lord by the mere confession of asking, "Who are you, Lord?' Through all his years of religious training Saul never experienced nor understood that the Lord was a light as bright as this.

The light blinded Saul, and he could not see for a few days. However,

God got his attention by replying, "This is Jesus, the one you persecute. Now get up and go into the city and you will be told what to do next."

Saul became the Apostle Paul and went on to lead the New Testament church and write many of the New Testament books. During one flash of absolute light, Paul's entire past, present, and future was revealed, and God's light of completeness healed one of the vilest religious leaders.

The table below captures the events in Paul's experience and can help your relate to your own moment of light that may be on its way.

Facts about Saul/Paul	What God and Light Did in Saul/Paul's Circumstance	Scripture Reference
Paul was a zealous religious murderer of Christians.	Instantaneously made him a completely new person past, present, and future.	Acts 7:58, Acts 9:1, Acts 9:13
Paul states that the light that knocked him off his horse was "around" him, and in one passage states it was a "complete" light.	Light formed a completeness around Saul. He was being healed from his past, present, and future. He was made a completely new man. The light reflected and refracted off his past, present, and future, possibly much like the crystals in the halo effect.	Acts 9:3, Acts 22:6, Acts 26:13
God cleansed his past for a greater purpose in his future.	When Christians heard that the murderer named Saul had been cleansed and forgiven, they argued with God. God told them, "He is now a chosen vessel unto God."	Acts 9:15, Acts 9:21
God revealed the true pearl in Saul via the light that flashed around Paul.	God's light in this process is one of the greatest human examples. It shows that God can take even his own irritants (a murderer of Christians) and find the pearl within them. This shows all of us greater hope!	Acts 9:15

Table 6.2: Defining Attributes of Saul/Paul's Encounter with Light

The story of the Apostle Paul should give great hope for every circumstance you may have been through. I am of the opinion that Paul had to see so much light at one time because he had so much past baggage. A sense of love by the local church group was not going to wipe out the fact he was killing Christians. Saul allowed God's light to shine through to pierce his past, present, and future so he could truly love the Lord with all his heart, mind, and soul. God's light is all empowering and transforming; it is what gave Paul the love he needed for the Jews and Gentiles as well as his enemies.

It is amazing how love is a natural outcome of God's light, but when we put love first or consider love a message all by itself, it is a backward message that disappoints many people. This is why Jesus stated in Matthew 5:16, "Let your light so shine before men that they may see good works and glorify your father in heaven." Jesus did not say, "Let your love so shine before men so they could see your good works." The reason that light comes first in the sequence is because light, not love, fulfills God's original purpose for the good works. Light in me allows people to give glory to God, not glory to me or my love. If people see my love and my good works, they will tend to give me the credit and the glory instead of God. If they see the light that is in me through Christ, they will give him the glory, knowing that my good works can come only through His light within me. The same concept is true with Paul. If he had been loved by a church group into forgiveness or relationship with Jesus, he would have quickly given thanks and glory to the church or people instead of God.

We are getting into the heart of this chapter, the transforming power of God's light. In Paul's story of forgiveness, we find in Acts 9:9–15 that a fellow Christian, Ananias, had been hurt by Paul's acts of murder and was not ready to forgive Paul and follow God's request to pray for Paul to be a blessing to the world. Nonetheless, the Lord's light also showed Ananias that even though he was offended and hurt by murder he could forgive Paul and endorse His new future. Once again, there are not many acts of forgiveness greater than forgiving someone who murdered your friends or family, but God's light is able to transcend the issues, circumstances, times and our individual purposes to give every human hope. God is willing to forgive perpetrators who went as far as torture or murder, and He gives people who were violated against in such cases the ability to forgive the perpetrators. A person no longer has to be bitter over past violations; this is amazing, as bitterness is like drinking your own poison and expecting the other person to die.

Consider the fact that the reason it is so hard to forgive your trespassers is because you are trying to forgive them in your own human love versus letting God forgive them in His transforming light. When God forgives them, and you, like Ananias, believe it, you could possibly see God's reflection in the person God forgave. Ananias had to pray for Paul and look at his newfound light reflected in Paul. If we let God forgive them through His light, your human love and forgiveness can follow. Also, if you follow scripture, which says, "Do unto others as you would have them do unto you," then you should believe God for their forgiveness with the same belief you had for God to shed light and forgiveness on your issues.

As followers of Christ we must attempt to follow His actions. Jesus was violated in the most severe and traumatic manner before He was killed, but even after the violations of His name, identity, physical being, position, flesh, blood, and pride, He still prayed for his violators and killers to be forgiven. Christ experienced violations until death to help fulfill the passage; He felt our infirmities and was tempted in every way we have been but without sin (Hebrews 4:15; Matthew 8:17). Jesus suffered many violations to relate to ours.

We will not know until we get to heaven the depths of pain and experiences that Christ went through between His death and resurrection. We do not know exactly what happened during that three-day period that Jesus went to the heart of the earth (Matthew 12:40) to set captives free. However, what we do know is that Jesus experienced all levels of our infirmities and overcame all dominions, powers, and authorities and even conquered death's sting. He traveled the distance for you and me so we can truly claim that by His stripes we are healed!

> But he was pierced for our transgressions, he was crushed for our iniquities; the punishment that brought us peace was upon him, and by his wounds we are healed. (Isaiah 53:5)

The biblical reality is that Jesus allowed Himself to be violated to give us confidence that no matter how we were violated, we, like Christ, can ask for forgiveness. This in no way invalidates what people have experienced or have gone through. There will always be people who experience unbelievably traumatic setbacks that are unique and personal. In no way is it God's design to invalidate their situations or circumstances by merely implying they were not as bad as what Jesus suffered. Some people who cannot see the fullness of Christ's travels and experiences conclude that Christ could not have experienced what they did. However, it is not Christ's purpose to have humanity compare the severity of their wounds to His; it is also not Christ's desire to expect me to experience what He went through before forgiving others.

Christ states that we are not in a war of flesh and blood but battle principalities, powers, the rulers of the darkness of this world, and spiritual wickedness in high places. If I make my issues about violations of the flesh, I may be missing the real cause and consequences of the violation that are in the spiritual realm (Ephesians 6:10). I am so thankful that through Christ God provided a means for us all to be healed in numerous belief systems based on the various things Christ went through. People can choose to:

1. accept with childlike faith the fact that by Christ's stripes they can be healed from anything! I believe God is well pleased with this kind of childlike faith.
2. focus on the extreme death and violations that Christ suffered and see that He set an example for them; therefore, they too can forgive their accusers or violators.
3. understand that Jesus traveled to the depths of the earth and overcame every evil power, dominion, principality, and death and that He overcame and paid the price for their wounds, transgressions, and transgressors and therefore have faith to forgive and receive forgiveness.
4. believe with childlike faith that in some supernatural way in the spiritual realm of light Jesus truly experienced everyone's infirmities, and believe that if He walked their walk without sin, then they too can make an attempt to forgive and be forgiven.

5. believe with complete confidence that if Jesus is Light, He can travel through their pasts, presents, and futures and experience everything they did and take claim that He was personally tempted in every way they were. They can believe that the Light of the World transforms, heals, cleanses, and forgives. And with this resurrected Christ living in them, they can forgive and be forgiven.

The belief people use to allow them to be healed and forgive others is of less concern than the central reality and truth, which is that Christ's blood removed everyone's sins. Jesus's light is powerful enough to shine in each circumstance to ensure His death and resurrection were not in vain.

You have just listened and processed some of the most simple yet most powerful promises found in the Bible. God's light shines in such a way that we along with Him can transcend our past issues into our future! Allowing God's light to transcend these issues allows them to pass through the illumination of God's light for complete healing. I, like the halo, can form the completeness that God always intended for me.

Remember, the two great attributes of light are speed and illumination. This self-completeness includes my past, present, and future, which are connected very closely to the three things God said we are to worship him with: our hearts, minds, and souls. Unfortunately, during most of my Christian walk I had been exposed only to the heart side of my life. About six years ago I learned I had developed only one-third of the aspects God was looking for me to serve and worship him with. I strived, functioned, and operated on Christian love, God's love, the Church's love, the pastor's love, and my husband's love to the point that my love "balloon" was ready to burst because I did not develop my mind and my soul. Without developing my mind and my soul, how could I truly love God with all my heart, mind, and soul?

I realized that until God's light came in its fullness, my mind did not want to deal with the past, and therefore my soul could not encompass my own fullness of whom God wanted and created me to be. This kind of behavior adds to the disappointments that love-based relationships bring. The true light allowed me to see my entire heart, mind, and soul as the completeness of whom God always desired me to be. I have forgiven myself and my violators and transgressors, stopped operating off emotion, and allowed God's light to reflect and refract off all things in my life.

Unit 2

The Principles and Keys to Seeing Heaven 3.0

Now that we have taken a look at the many attributes of seeing more of the kingdom of God and heavenly aspects, we will look at things that normally hinder us from reaching our fullest potential and seeing the greatest realms of God. Chapters 7 through 14 are biblical principles to ensure we all have the greatest opportunities to see everything God has promised!

- **Chapter 7:** The Law of Refraction and Reflection
- **Chapter 8:** The Principle of Illusion of Knowledge and Time
- **Chapter 9:** The Law of Reference-Point Living—The OODA Loop
- **Chapter 10:** The Principle of the Enigma Experience
- **Chapter 11:** The Principle of the Merchant and Pearl
- **Chapter 12:** The Principle of Thanksgiving Worship
- **Chapter 13:** The Principle of Clouds: Keeping Your Head in the Clouds
- **Chapter 14:** Fearfully and Wonderfully Made

Science has found that nothing can disappear without a trace. Nature does not know extinction. All it knows is transformation. If God applies the fundamental principle to the most minute and insignificant parts of the universe, doesn't it make sense to assume that He applies it to the masterpiece of His creation—the human soul? I think it does. —Dr. Werner von Braun

CHAPTER 7

THE LAW OF REFRACTION AND REFLECTION

Healing Your Past with Your Future

This is the message we have heard from him and declare to you: God is light; in him, there is no darkness at all.
—1 John 1:5

There's much more for me included in Christ's salvation than merely a paid ticket to heaven. There is victory over present circumstances if I am willing to accept it.
—Matilda Nordtvedt

Reflection occurs when light bounces off an object and comes back to the source of light. When the sun hits flat metal, the light rays reflect off the metal back at the sun, giving a reflection from the sun. Refraction is where the source of light bounces off an object, and depending on the angle and composition of the object, passes through one dimension and out another. For instance, when light hits a prism, it passes through one side and comes out the other in a potentially new form of light ray(s). This concept of reflection and refraction is what is happening when we open up our past, present, and future as a three-dimensional view for God's light to pass through. His light can pass through my present circumstances, and if I let His light shine on my past, it will illuminate my past as well as my future on the other side, making me personally complete. However, if I choose to shut down areas of my past, the light of God cannot come through and expose, illuminate, heal, and bring them cleanly into my future, so I remain incomplete.

You may ask how this reflection and refraction take place to heal your past and future. Think about the many dreams you have. If you are mindful of your dreams, you will notice you have dreams that include childhood memories, past memories in general, present circumstances, and future events. All these dreams (most allowed by God) are a manner in which God can show us the past, present, and future to allow us to reflect on the past and refract into the future. In fact, the refraction is why many futuristic dreams may seem so strange and distorted. God gives dreams to help you get into the right future. Considering that this concept is so simple yet so revealing, we will continue as we have with a few more biblical examples that will help you take special notice of God's light as well as His transcending power from the past into the future.

Biblical Example 1: Acts 7:54–59

In Acts 7, Stephen was being stoned and killed by the religious leaders, including Saul. Stephen takes his stoning with great grace because he did something many of us refuse or don't know how to do: he allowed his reflection and refraction to shine in the midst of the circumstance:

But Stephen, full of the Holy Spirit, looked up to heaven and saw the glory of God, and Jesus standing at the right hand of God. "Look," he said. "I see heaven open and the Son of Man standing at the right hand of God." While they were stoning him, Stephen prayed, "Lord Jesus, receive my spirit." Then he fell on his knees and cried out, "Lord, do not hold this sin against them." When he had said this, he fell asleep. (Acts 7:55, 56, 59, 60)

These words are powerful because Stephen allowed himself to look toward heaven and reflect as well as refract back and forth with heaven. Before they stoned Stephen, he was able to see into heaven and view the glory of God, which also reflected back toward him, giving him the strength for the moment as well as the willingness to forgive them in advance of what they were doing. Imagine this kind of power that allows you to see into a circumstance, view heavenly details, and reach into the future and forgive someone who is stoning you to death. Most of us cannot forgive people until after the violation has been completed against us, but Stephen did it before they completed violating him, right in the midst of the circumstance. This is not love; this is the power of light! There was no lovefest going on in this circumstance; it was a lightfest in which the power, glory, and light of God opened up to Stephen. In a split second he was able to reflect on his recent sermon (Acts 7:2–54), and refract into his future to see his position with Christ in heaven, giving him the ability to say "forgive" the sin.

Biblical Example 2

Before we get into the exact biblical example, let me give you some background on the word "quicken," used to illustrate the concept of speeding up something, making someone more alert or aware about something or bringing something to life. Scripture uses this word in Romans 8:11 (KJV) to demonstrate an experience we all can have when we let the same Spirit that raised Christ from the dead dwell in us. This is why it is not strange that Stephen and millions of other martyrs can joyfully be killed. They are experiencing a "quickening" or "coming alive" feeling that comes from the same Spirit that raised Christ from the dead. What an awesome thought to know that not only was Jesus raised, resurrected, and made alive, but we may also get to experience this at times.

> And if the Spirit of him who raised Jesus from the dead is living in you, he who raised Christ from the dead will also give life to your mortal bodies through his Spirit, who lives in you. (Romans 8:11)

This passage verifies that Jesus was raised from the dead by the Spirit of God. Just prior to being raised from the dead Jesus uttered, "It is finished!" Many people oversimplify this and say it was in reference to His death, but the reality is that he was just made alive again. What He was more than likely saying was the very things he saw just prior to the Spirit raising him from the dead. The things he saw were probably the kind of things that Stephen witnessed just prior to His death and then some! What Christ saw was so powerful, wonderful, and majestic that darkness invaded the land for three hours, an earthquake split the temple curtain in two, and many dead saints arose from their graves (Matthew 27:52–53).

Not only did the Spirit raise Christ from the dead, but the Spirit also raised many who had been dead. At that moment they got out of their graves and walked into Jerusalem. Yes, this fact is often overlooked, but it is right in scripture. The Spirit of the Living God was quickening this special moment in time to allow the real story, His story, to be visualized by His Son. More than likely what Jesus saw in a split, quickening moment was the experience of things becoming fast motion and slow motion at the same time. He probably saw in a split second the entire past, present, and future flash with a bright light that allowed him to endure the pain He was going through. Within a split second he saw the reconnection of humanity all the way from the history of humanity through present day humanity and out into the future of humanity all being saved by His personal sacrifice. When He saw this, He was able to say, "It is finished." God and Christ, who are light, traveled in that moment throughout history and into the future to save each and every soul ever born and who were to be born. It was the greatest quickening experience known to humanity.

That same Spirit that raised Christ from the dead desires to quicken your life, which includes your past, present, and future, but will you let Him? Jesus had to first become obedient unto death before He saw His quickening moment. You too must become obedient unto the death of your sins and people who have sinned against you in order to reconnect your past, present, and future. This will be your own quickening moment.

As you recall, we started this journey with the photos of the halo effect, where light is able to shine in a complete circle around all aspects of ice crystals in a cloud. Are you ready to let God's light shine into all past, present, and future aspects of your life to make you who you were always created to be? You cannot forget your past if you want to get to your future; you need to heal and reconnect your past with your future. In this manner God receives all the glory.

Spend the next few days reviewing this chapter and taking notes on your own completeness. Seek after God's answers and light to begin to let God know you are thankful for His provision to deal with your past, present, and future. Do some examination of the happiest people you know. Usually the people who are the happiest are not those who've made no serious mistakes or have not had serious violations committed against them. In fact, you will most often find just the opposite is true.

CHAPTER 8

THE PRINCIPLE OF ILLUSION OF KNOWLEDGE AND TIME

*Listen to me, you islands; hear this, you distant nations:
Before I was born the LORD called me; from my birth he
has made mention of my name.*

—Isaiah 49:1

*Time and space are modes by which we think and not
conditions in which we live.*

—Albert Einstein

In the introduction we discussed the advancement of technology during the last fifty years. The generations of technology advances went from dial-up phones and citizen band radios to wireless cell phones, Smartphones, etc. The underlying generations of technology advances such as 2G, 3G, and now 4G networks allow for the transmission of more data and information.

During the same fifty years other transformations happened. For instance, baby boomers (born in the 1950s and 1960s) were taught at home and at school that the Russians were coming. Throughout their childhoods they were taught to fear Russia and to wait for the inevitable day the Russians would invade America. The Russians never came. This does not mean it was not a fear during the Cold War era, but it is a reminder how our minds can be trained and captivated with fears and worries.

Technology will continue to advance, but the fear of who is after "me" or "America" has only become different people or different demographic, political, religious, cultic, or hate groups. Our civilization in many ways has advanced in access to knowledge but has remained relatively primitive when it comes to the concepts of survival and fear. Possibly we are even more fearful now because the bad people we fear have greater advancements in technology to carry out their causes. Our chances for survival are growing grimmer. For millions of people, the grim reaper is always pounding at their doors.

On one hand our civilization and knowledge has advanced during the past twenty years further than we could have ever imagined. Unfortunately, we still wrestle with people's fear factors, circumstances, or events that can reshape our worldviews. The struggle I have in my own life is that I can swing great distances in my imagination between belief and fear. In one day I can swing between a belief system in which I am on the verge of doing something spectacular in the world, all the way to a belief system in which I fear being wiped out financially due to an economic crisis. For some people these kind of mental swings occur fairly regularly and develop an up-and-down pattern in their minds. I realize I must daily if not hourly renew my mind to the right balance so I do not swing too far in either direction. The inability to control these potential swings will prevent me from developing the perfect direction for my life (Romans 12:2).

This pattern of swinging between greater advances and greater fears develops a delusion or false sense of advancing our lives. If you are human and live in the same society in which I live, you will admit that you also deal with these swings in beliefs. You may also admit you have experienced days when you have never felt more unsure, more confused, more depressed, more tired, more financially unstable, more vulnerable, more fearful, and more uneasy about the future than ever. Yet you would share that you have had these times interlaced with feelings of great victory, encouragement, financial freedom, peace, and joy. These interwoven frequencies of great victory and great defeat occur in such a manner that we can become delusional toward what is factual.

Picture the swings of behavior of a modern teenager who owns a Smartphone and accesses Facebook and gets or sends text messages every minute. This teenager is constantly transferring bits of new information every sixty seconds, yet the world around him or her at school may be in turmoil due to teacher layoffs, bullying, etc. There is a pendulum that allows teenagers to ignore the reality of fearful things around them because they are being updated by their friends every sixty seconds. The technology advances gives a perception of a "false world" around us. The timetable of schools in budget crises, teachers' contract debates, and bullying have been occurring and escalating over a period of time that is more like watching grass grow, but a sixty-second update from friends is frequent enough to pretend that the world is more normal than the facts or problems right around the corner.

The focus and frequency of social media updates allow people to avoid the life-changing issues happening around them. What this creates is lapses of time in space whereby events seem to be out of sync or appear to have happened overnight when in fact we were just unaware of the updates that were more infrequent than the sixty-second updates. Many people are living in trances whereby they feel like they have missed out on events or times that suddenly are the real deal.

On a larger scale, imagine a country in the Middle East called Libya, Egypt, or Tunisia, where the oppression of the rulers was always on the people's minds, a place where citizens were often prevented from using new technologies and social media tools such as Facebook, Twitter, etc. In their worlds every sixty-second interval was filled with thoughts of dictators and oppression and not text messages from friends. However, when the use of social media and connection to other parts of the world suddenly became available to them during the last two years, these countries experienced a complete turnover as young people were quickly enlightened to the realities that other people on the other side of the world had freedoms they could also possess. This occurred in these countries, and the world was astonished to witness the fall of three to four countries in 2011. The young people of these countries made a decision to be enlightened and to turn away from the dictators and tyrants they had been oppressed by. Unfortunately, the quickness in which the implosion occurred may not have resulted in a better outcome.

This new enlightenment was no different than the first-century Gospel in which young, new believers in the new generation of religion quickly sacrifices their lives in exchange for the new liberty or freedom from the situations that had oppressed them for so long. The 2011 implosions in Libya, Tunisia, and Egypt came suddenly and unexpectedly due to new generations of knowledge. Through the use of small but incredible devices that bring enlightenment, knowledge, and newfound friends, third-world citizens are startling the world by toppling their oppressive kingdoms. In essence, young people from the other parts of the world were traveling via YouTube, social media, and texting within a few seconds. These quick bursts of knowledge and virtual travel are specifically what Daniel saw in Daniel 12:4: "Knowledge will increase and many people will go to and fro."

We are living in times of increased knowledge as Daniel 12:4 describes. However, the knowledge and quick access to information from different parts of the world through flight or technology can cause mismanaged outcomes. On one hand we may swing between teenagers oblivious to their surroundings to conquering kingdoms. In other scenarios we may use the advancements to partake in a citywide "occupy" demonstration or begin a "sexting" affair that destroys our reputations or marriages. Technological advancements can build or destroy relationships, theories, and kingdoms in less time than ever before. Our civilization has created an environment in which on any day we can swing tree to tree like Tarzan or get caught in quicksand that consumes our emotions, relationships, finances, homes, and futures.

These images I am giving you should be alarming to us all. My solution, by the way, is far from the easy way out; it is to bail out on the new advances in technology. My recommended solution is hopefully more spiritually sound and profound. Let me explain by giving an example of a young athlete who becomes a pro and goes from playing college football for free to becoming a $30-million-a-year player at age twenty-two. That athlete will have gone through multiple generations of income growth in twenty-four hours in spite of the fact that his character cannot grow four generations overnight. This concept is illustrated in Figure 8.1 and could also apply to businesspeople, lottery winners, and drug dealers who experience quick spurts of success without the ability to grow their characters and senses of honor.

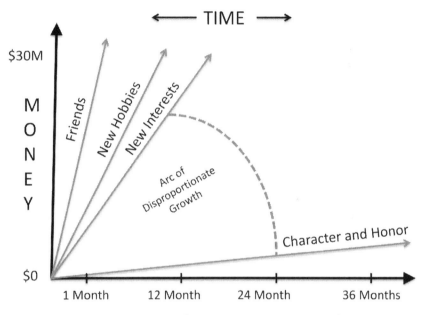

Figure 8.1: Arc of Disproportionate Growth

The athlete who quickly goes from zero to $30 million a year will be greatly tested in the areas of character and honor. He will suddenly have all kinds of new friends, interests, and hobbies that fit his new salary. Unfortunately, the friends, hobbies, and interests will develop at a rate faster than character and honor can normally develop. If that athlete can expand and grow his character to match his newfound hobbies, friends, and interests, all may be well. You can see from the illustration in Figure 8.1 that there will be a mismatch I call the "arc of disproportionate growth" that will develop over time. There is a mismatch between the critical element of character and honor that creates issues over time. Some people will have already developed their characters and senses of honor at an earlier stage in their lives and avoided the arc of disproportionate growth. History has shown that tangible things like money, friends, and hobbies are more believable than the traits of character and honor. In fact, character and honor will appear as invisible until issues arise that reveal the underdevelopment of character and honor.

Now let's go back to the reality of what has happened over time in the area of spiritual growth. Figure 8.2 illustrates a similar pattern of activity when knowledge increases over time versus money. Spiritual knowledge increased at a much slower rate than we advanced our knowledge of bigger and better churches, improved communication through mobile technologies, enhancements to people's abilities and beauty, and life-enhancing pharmaceuticals. Over the last ten or twenty years we have increased the generations of enhancements by a factor of four. The enhancements all make us sound better, look better, feel better (at times), communicate better, and even transfer information better. We have beautified many of the aspects of life as each generation of enhancement has been discovered.

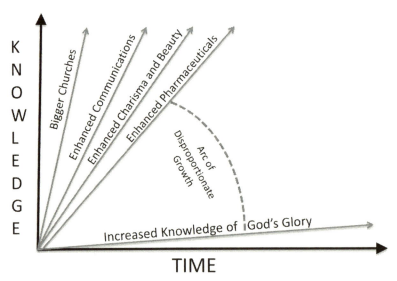

Figure 8.2: Arc of Disproportionate Growth

Unfortunately, we developed the same arc of disproportionate growth as the athlete or lottery winner. At the same time we saw a four-times generational enhancement in technology, pharmaceuticals, beauty, and buildings we never saw an increase in generational knowledge of God. The same character and honor flaw so easy to see in the athlete's arc of disproportionate growth applies to many people in the area of spiritual growth. This concept helps explain why we see so much of the following:

+ People who believe that phone signals can travel through space and globally hit every square inch of every square mile but think that God's spirit or angels are distant and unable to travel to meet their immediate needs.

+ People who started affairs online or through "sexting" but no longer believe God is real or applicable to their lives. These electronic communications have become more sensual, enticing, entrancing, and stimulating than communication with God Himself.

+ Clergy who have become addicted to sex and drugs and have lost their positions of authority while at the same time stopped believing in the miracles of God and even preached that the miracles of God were only for the early church.

+ People who are more afraid of losing their health benefits than losing their relationships with God.

+ Many church groups whose members experience a higher rate of divorce than the average, unchurched population.

+ Clergy who fall out, burn out, spin out, and bail out.

+ Young people for whom prescription drugs have become a debilitating addiction because many don't need to go any farther than their grandparents' home-grown "stash" to get a fix.

+ People who rely on medications and implants for hours of nonstop sexual satisfaction while they can't find ten minutes to seek God.

+ Clergy and coaches who have molested the innocent without many people blinking an eye.

+ People buying into fantasies that their teeth can be whiter, their body parts enhanced, and that they can become more stimulating with just pills or procedures.

I could go on about how mixed up our society has gotten as we advanced generations of knowledge in the fields of technology, beauty, and pharmaceuticals while never advancing to new generations of knowledge of God's beauty, ability, miracles, and kingdom. On almost every topic we have advanced wisdom, knowledge, technology, and the benefits thereof, but we allow our spiritual growth to stop at a basic and rudimentary knowledge of heavenly things. There is a drastic gap (the arc of disproportionate growth) between the greatness of God and our daily lives of advancements. We have squeezed God out of our advancement equation.

Many people have been stuck at the Heaven 1.0 level. It is no wonder God has entered the scene and poured out His Spirit through dreams, visions, and out-of-body experiences for people. God's natural way for humans to increase their generations of knowledge has been to ask and seek by knocking on heaven's door. This method is well pleasing to him and allows us to advance at the same generational increases as the things of this world. It has always been God's desire for us to increase in knowledge and seek heavenly things.

Ask and it will be given to you; seek and you will find; knock and the door will be opened to you. For everyone who asks receives; he who seeks finds; and to him who knocks, the door will be opened." (Matthew 7:7–8)

And we pray this in order that you may live a life worthy of the Lord and may please him in every way: bearing fruit in every good work, growing in the knowledge of God. (Colossians 1:10)

Since, then, you have been raised with Christ, set your hearts on things above, where Christ is seated at the right hand of God. Set your minds on things above, not on earthly things. (Colossian 3:1–2)

Imagine the generational advances in our knowledge of God if we would invest the same kind of seeking, asking, and knocking that we do with all other aspects of our lives. We would be amazed at the amount of God's glory we would see if we asked and knocked, and in return that glory would allow us to see the kingdom of God in more-advanced ways.

Many people have given more credibility, trust, and confidence to every facet of life and just assumed that God was inferior to advancing His kingdom. This arc of disproportionate growth has caused an almost irreversible effect on our generation. As an example, reports indicate that 15 to 25 percent of young ladies in high schools cut their wrists as a means to draw enough blood to release their emotional pains. The reality is simple: they see blood as a replacement for the blood of Christ in a warped sense due to the false imagery they get from the advancements in media that show vampires and other blood-exalting behavior patterns that go against the knowledge of God. Simply put, they have been confused and disillusioned by the four-times growth of enhancements of beauty, media, propaganda, and false body parts.

It should be noted that young churched ladies are not immune to this behavior as most attend church at a place that has not shown the power of God's generational advancements to meet the needs of people today. This same behavior extends to marriage within the church where modern programs and enhancements in books, marriage seminars, counselors, and marital pastors have been placed as the altar in the church versus the power of the blood of Christ. Marriages have become idols before God.

Modern-day church leaders and the missions of their churches have put people in a sleepless slumber because they have not advanced the kingdom of God. Rather, they have advanced the methods, buildings, music, worship, beauty, and vitamin-packed messages in place of the knowledge, power, glory, honor, and character of God. They have allowed generational advancements in everything but God. They have fallen behind a few generations of revelation that pertains to the power of the kingdom of God.

Summary

We have been deceived for a few generations to believe that time and knowledge never change as they pertain to the kingdom of God and heaven when the reality is that things are progressing at a pace at which the entire earth will be filled with the knowledge of the glory of God. During this same time we have put far more hope in the advancements that we could actually touch and utilize.

I want to go back to the whisper I shared in the introduction. God is allowing an unprecedented window of opportunity to all people to gather glimpses of His glory that exceed the enhancements the world has offered to people. However, it will require that people be willing to give Him the credit due His name. God is willing to show His invisible aspects that are far greater than our visible aspects.

> For since the creation of the world God's invisible qualities—his eternal power and divine nature—have been clearly seen, being understood from what has been made, so that men are without excuse. For although they knew God, they neither glorified him as God nor gave thanks to him, but their thinking became futile and their foolish hearts were darkened. (Romans 1:20–21)

CHAPTER 9

THE LAW OF REFERENCE-POINT LIVING: THE OODA LOOP

I have spoken to you of earthly things and you do not believe; how then will you believe if I speak of heavenly things?

—John 3:12

We can enjoy Heaven now. We can have half of the enjoyment ahead of time by looking forward to it, thinking about it, reading about it and anticipating it.

—David Brandt Berg

During the 1950s, USAF colonel and fighter pilot John Boyd earned the nickname "Forty Second Boyd" due to his impeccable record of defeating opposing fighter pilots in forty seconds or less. Boyd also became known as the pilot who changed the art of war by articulating how he was able to conquer his enemy so quickly and bring U.S. fighter pilots to a 10-to-one win ratio over the superior Russian MiG-16 fighter jets. Even though the American F-86 was inferior to the MiG-16, the new art of war that Forty Second Boyd developed was encompassed in his theory called the OODA loop. Boyd's theory was that those who can quickly adjust to stimuli or challenging circumstances in quick and repeatable manners have a greater chance of overcoming their oncoming challenges. Humans can respond to stimuli or challenges in about 220 milliseconds, but few people learn the discipline of repeating this response over and over again to overcome obstacles that oppose them. Boyd concluded that if he was able to observe the challenges or stimuli in a continuous, ongoing manner he could then reassemble all the necessary reference points in order to outmaneuver his opponents.

When flying a fighter jet at high speed at high altitudes, a pilot must be capable of readjusting all the reference points he is seeing in real time over and over. When a fighter pilot observes multiple disconnected stimuli or circumstances in the sky, he must instantly reassemble the disconnected pieces into a reference point of truth on which he can act. Doing so allows pilots to quickly orient themselves to what they are seeing so they can make a decision and act upon that decision. This Observation–Orientation–Decide–Act (OODA) looping of the mind may sound somewhat obvious, but imagine doing this every 220 milliseconds when in a life-and-death circumstance such as fighter pilots face. Pilots who could continually loop, or repeat, this mental yet visual reassembling of different stimuli in the quickest and most consistent fashion usually win combats in the sky. Forty Second Boyd was so good at this repeatable reassembling process that he was guaranteed a win against all his opposing pilots in forty seconds or less. His theory was that the quicker he was able to reassemble the pieces, the more confusion he placed in the opposing pilots' abilities to reassemble their pieces of their flight-or-fight environment. The best fighter pilots were those who could imagine and reassemble all the individual pieces into a singular object of truth, those who could see the following four individual items in the air and could within milliseconds envision a snowmobile from the four completely independent pieces without ever having seen a snowmobile before. This kind of observation and orientation is what made the air fights more of an art than a science.

1. A pair of handlebars

2. A toboggan

3. An engine

4. A windshield

The ability for pilots to visually and mentally reassemble the pieces of stimuli they see while fighting is an ongoing process Boyd perfected and proved true for himself. Eventually, Boyd went on to articulate the OODA loop for other pilots. Below are the four pieces of the OODA loop along with a simple diagram in figure 9.1 and more-complex diagram in figure 9.2.

1. **Observe:** Collect current information from as many sources as practically possible.

2. **Orient:** Analyze this information and use it to update your current reality.

3. **Decide:** Determine a course of action.

4. **Act:** Follow through on your decision.

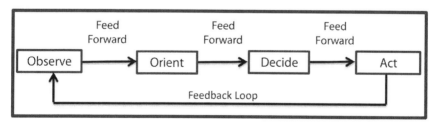

Figure 9.1: A Simple Illustration of the OODA Loop

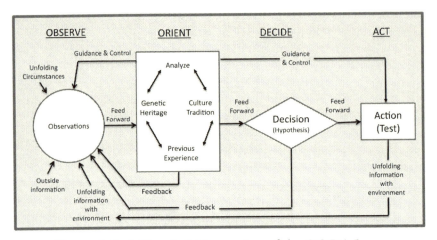

Figure 9.2: A Detailed Illustration of the OODA Loop

In its simplest form, the OODA loop is the art of defining reference points that can help orient yourself to facts or truths in order to decide on an action. Without reference points most people struggle with where to start making decisions from. Ever since Boyd's discovery, many other leaders have applied the theory to everyday scenarios whereby leaders must make quicker decisions.

A Personal Example of a Reference Point Living

During the years Pam and I were raising our two daughters, Jessica and Tiffany, we often went through moments when we felt inadequate and would question our abilities as parents. We had to adjust our thinking toward a known truth or reference point to avoid overreacting to our feelings of inadequacy or completely ignoring those feelings. Erring on the side of ignoring our feelings may have allowed us to become worse parents and to have brought guilt or conviction upon us years later. On the other hand, overreacting to our feelings may have forced us to over-adjust our parenting skills or to allow our children to leverage their disappointments toward us in a negative way. To avoid the mistake of over-adjusting our parenting skills we needed reference points that would quickly allow us to validate what kind of parents we were.

Below are the seven reference points Pam and I chose to measure our situation against:

1. Are we doing better than our parents did with us when we were children?
2. If we are doing better than our parents, are our children better off at this point in their lives than where we were at their age?
3. Are we in agreement with how we want to raise our children?
4. How have we let God manage these feelings in the past?
5. Do our current lives, attitudes, and situations please God?
6. Are we following the few biblical examples available for parents?
7. Are we avoiding other people's opinions and listening to good, solid advice?

We developed these reference points over a series of years once we realized there was no easy, proven formula for handling our feelings of inadequacy. After the third or fourth iteration we learned to quickly scan this list of multiple references to draw a conclusion if we were reacting to our feelings in a logical method. As our marriage progressed, our feelings of how well we were raising our family were solved in minutes rather than weeks. We were able to mentally orient ourselves to the reference points (objects) to give us some logic for decision making.

As Pam and I now look back over our child-rearing years, we realize that this type of reference-point living literally gave us the assurance and confidence we needed to avoid managing our parenting and marriage by feelings and emotions. It gave us logical proof points on how we were measuring up.

In essence, Pam and I were practicing the process that Forty Second Boyd was great at, the OODA loop.

1. **Observe** what we were feeling/seeing.
2. **Orient** ourselves to some basic reference points (seven in our case above).

3. **Decide** to what degree to adjust our parenting skills.
4. **Act** upon the decision to stay the course we were on or upon the new adjustment.

Few Measurements Available for Relationships and Spiritual Life

We realize early in life that most of our circumstances have reference points that allow us to operate with and adjust against, including:

- Taxpayers have tax brackets issued by the IRS to show how much they have to pay or get back.
- Car drivers have speed limits as reference points to know if they are above or below the speed limit.
- Education has grading systems to show how well students are doing.
- Golfers have scorecards with reference points that let them know if they are above or below par.
- Bowlers have reference points, their strikes and spares, to know how well they are doing during every bowling frame.
- For IQ testing we have reference points of above or below average.
- The U.S. Census Bureau gives us reference points about the average-size city, household income, counties, and states that are national reference points.
- The U.S. Department of Labor publishes high, low, and average salaries for most job classifications so we know where we are in reference to careers.

In many walks of life we have some fairly good reference points to measure against, which allow us to perform a very quick OODA loop of observing, orienting, deciding, and acting.

One of the sad facts of life very few people are willing to admit is that most issues among dysfunctional people, families, organizations, churches, businesses, and societies come directly from their inability to make decisions. The most dysfunctional people are those who can never make decisions. One of the main reasons most people can't make decisions is because they do not have enough reference points to measure their indecision against. This is extremely true when it comes to relationships, family matters, and spiritual matters. This is one of the reasons so many people get misaligned with the wrong friends, churches, organizations, and jobs. Worse yet, it is why they also stay in misaligned relationships, churches, organizations, and jobs.

The Spiritual Realm Dilemma

The OODA loop concept and other possible ideas for garnering reference points to help make decisions eventually becomes a practice that helps many people. Where this concept breaks down quickly is in spiritual, supernatural, and heavenly realms. Let's try a few examples that would be similar to a pilot imagining a snowmobile after seeing a handlebar, a windshield, a toboggan, and an engine. Imagine if I give you the following four spiritual items sets that include five spiritual stimuli or thoughts. Imagine what the five stimuli or thoughts in each set would produce. For instance, in Set 1 within Table 9.1, the five thoughts or pieces of information known as stimuli would/could allow me to construct or assemble the image of eternal life. What would a spiritual person construct or imagine if he or she tried to reassemble the five individual thoughts provided in sets 2 through 4 of Table 9.1.?

Set 1	Set 2	Set 3	Set 4
Grace of God	Miracles	Old men dreaming	Fiery eyes
Forgiveness	Keys to the kingdom	Young men having visions	Sound of many rushing waters
Salvation	Gifts of the Spirit	Children giving many prophecies	Brass feet
Thread of redemption	Works greater than Jesus	Servants giving many prophecies	Hair white as wool

Set 1	Set 2	Set 3	Set 4
Death	Conqueror	Signs and wonders in the heavens	Brass girdle
Eternal life	God's spiritual gifts and promises to believers	End-time promises (Acts 2:17–21)	What Christ looks like prior to His return (Rev. 1:15)

Table 9.1: OODA Loop (Answers are on the last page of this chapter)

Hopefully this simple yet frustrating test allows you to see that our ability to creatively imagine or assemble the thoughts or stimuli in the spiritual realm may be slightly harder, but why? The two obvious reasons are that the stimuli in the spiritual realm are more abstract and require the ability to mentally scan or recall passages from scripture. A third yet more delicate reason why spiritual thoughts, concepts, or stimuli are difficult to process is due to the imagery that was created in our minds as young children concerning spiritual things we learned from Sunday school, videos of God, and deeply engrained doctrine from church, parents, and siblings. The power of our imagination is often tied directly to what has been placed at the center of what I call a personal truth serum. Our truth serum, our belief, plays a large part in what we imagine or construct when seeing or hearing certain stimuli or thoughts.

Just so you do not get discouraged but realize that the spiritual connections are more difficult, let's try some stimuli or thoughts from everyday life. Table 9.2 includes four more sets of thoughts that should produce outcomes.

Set 1	Set 2	Set 3	Set 4
Pink Slip	April 15	Proud of my daughter	Spouse has been frustrated in marriage for a few years

Set 1	Set 2	Set 3	Set 4
Bad economy	Tax tables have changed	GPA of 3.5	A notice from a lawyer
Reduction in the workforce	Money being taken out of my paychecks is not enough	My daughter is a senior in college	Romance and communication have been minimal
Company's revenues are down	One of my children is no longer in college	An invitation was sent to our closest friends and family members	Strange stares and avoidance by my spouse
Called into boss's office	My itemized deductions are 50 percent less than last year	Cleaning up the house	My mother-in-law called to ask if I was okay

Table 9.2: OODA Loop (Answers are on the last page of this chapter)

Let's try another set of four sets of five stimuli or concepts to see how well you are grasping why it is more difficult to assemble the pieces in the kingdom of God or spiritual realm.

Set 1	Set 2	Set 3	Set 4
Invisible aspect of Christ	A thief in the night	Rapture	No more tears
Eye has not seen nor ear heard of the great things God has prepared.	The days of Noah	Tribulation	No more death

Set 1	Set 2	Set 3	Set 4
Angel visits me and I could not tell if I was in a dream or not.	Dreams, visions, and prophecies	Three and a half years	Paradise
Whether I was in body or out of body I knew not.	Signs and wonders in the heavens	Two witnesses	Judgment seat
I was taken in spirit to another place.	Hearts failing for fear	Meet the Lord in the air	Streets of gold

Table 9.3: OODA Loop (Answers are on the last page of this chapter)

There are probably many reasons why the spiritual areas of life are more difficult to base a reference point system on, and here are just a few of them:

1. Most people are not open-minded enough to develop reference points in these areas because their traditional views are the reference points they have and will always choose to have, and their denomination has blinded them to any new reference points.
2. There are more opinions than facts concerning the spiritual aspects of life.
3. Spiritually related items are generally abstract and difficult to draw quick, easy, or consistent reference points from.
4. Some people have abused logic and have drawn reference points that do not align with the Bible.
5. The physical realm of our lives predominantly absorbs the majority of mind, will, and emotions. Assuming our minds are already occupied regularly with all our concerns, worries, and time, there is less time and energy to connect the spiritual reference points of life.

No matter what the exact reason is for our inability to draw reference points around spiritual things, the spiritual realm is consistently real and meant to be understood, experienced, and enjoyed. This form of drawing reference points in the spiritual realm is the exact topic Jesus and Nicodemus discussed. Nicodemus was trying to get a reference point about Jesus from an earthly perspective, while Jesus was trying to give Nicodemus a reference point about heavenly and spiritual perspectives. This is why Jesus told Nicodemus, "If I have told you of earthly things and you do not believe, how will you believe if I tell you heavenly things?" (John 3:12).

Think through the spiritual realms of life and try to figure out why spiritual things are more difficult to draw reference points around. After you spend a few minutes rationalizing the reasons, consider why most people who state they have seen, experienced, or witnessed a spiritual journey such as an out-of-body experience or a vision from heaven or hell were many times in life-and-death situations. Why do people in life-defying circumstances start seeing the spiritual side of life? I believe it is as simple as the following reasons:

1. The earthly issues they were dealing with suddenly no longer matter as much. When they cross that threshold they start to see the spiritual reference points that were always real but blocked from view by the daily grind and issues of life.
2. All the childhood beliefs, traditions, doctrines, and religions suddenly are overridden by the spiritual realm they sense, and they finally see the invisible aspects that have always been around but blocked from view because of traditions, doctrines, or religions.
3. The spiritual life is as real as the physical life, but many people never want to see it until something threatens, takes away, or removes physical life. It's amazing how heaven opens up and shows us heavenly and spiritual things when we are shut down from an earthly perspective.

The Apostle Paul was attempting to orient people to the spiritual aspects of life and gave us some of the following scripture passages as reference points to connect to the spiritual realms of reality:

Since, then, you have been raised with Christ, set your hearts on things above, where Christ is seated at the right hand of God. Set your minds on things above, not on earthly things. (Colossians 3:1–2)

Do not conform any longer to the pattern of this world, but be transformed by the renewing of your mind. Then you will be able to test and approve what God's will is-his good, pleasing and perfect will. (Romans 12:1–12) (Note: Paul is instructing us to daily realign our reference points by renewing our mind away from the worldly concerns and be transformed.)

He is the image of the invisible God, the firstborn over all creation. For by him all things were created: things in heaven and on earth, visible and invisible, whether thrones or powers or rulers or authorities; all things were created by him and for him. He is before all things, and in him all things hold together. (Colossians 1:15–17)

They were talking with each other about everything that had happened. As they talked and discussed these things with each other, Jesus himself came up and walked along with them; but they were kept from recognizing him. (Luke 24:14–16)

In Luke 24:14–16 we are given clear evidence that Jesus, the kingdom of God, angels, and the supernatural can at times be right in front of us but we can't see them because God is withholding them from our view or our concerns are preventing us from seeing things as they really are.

This chapter is intended to get you to understand that the spiritual and heavenly things are every bit as real as the earthly things, but we must develop a sense of awareness, appreciation, and respect for these aspects of life. The whole concept is somewhat of an enigma in that whatever we start to focus on is what we start seeing, and what we start seeing is what we start believing, and what we start believing is where we attach our thoughts, attentions, and energies.

Answers to Table 9.1:

Eternal life	God's spiritual gifts and promises to believers	End-time promises (Acts 2:17–21)	What Christ looks like prior to His return (Rev. 1:15)

Answers to Table 9.2:

I'm getting laid off.	I have to pay my taxes.	We are having a graduation party for my daughter's college graduation.	My spouse wants a divorce.

Answers to Table 9.3:

The supernatural activities of believers	The signs of the end times (Mat. 24)	The rapture	Paradise or heaven

CHAPTER 10

THE PRINCIPLE OF THE ENIGMA EXPERIENCE

"The eye is the lamp of the body. If your eyes are good, your whole body will be full of light. But if your eyes are bad, your whole body will be full of darkness. If then the light within you is darkness, how great is that darkness!"
                                                —Matthew 6:22-23

The faster we move in mind, body, thought, or spirit, the more of the impossible we are allowed to see.
                                                —Michael L. Mathews

The word "enigma" means a puzzling or inexplicable occurrence or situation. The Bible is filled with enigmas. A few of the thousands of scripture verses that could be classified as enigmas include:

> Now we see but a poor reflection as in a mirror; then we shall see face to face. Now I know in part; then I shall know fully, even as I am fully known. (1 Corinthians 13:12)

> The light of the body is the eye, if your eye is single your whole body will be full of light, but if your eye be evil, thy whole body shall be full of darkness, and how great is that darkness. (Matthew 6:22–23)

> The eyes of your understanding be enlightened; that you may know what is the hope of his calling and what the riches of the glory of his inheritance in the saints. (Ephesians 1:18–19)

The Bible as well as our everyday lives includes many enigmas that we usually contemplate and solve. In fact, for unsaved people the whole idea of salvation is a puzzle or even foolishness: "But we preach Christ crucified: a stumbling block to Jews and foolishness to Gentiles" (1 Corinthians 1:23). Taking the meaning of enigma one step further, we would be entertaining the word "mystery." As it relates to understanding the fullness of the Gospel and the kingdom, the word "mystery" appears thirty-eight times. The Apostle Paul solved many of the mysteries and shared them in the New Testament in order to make them comprehensible.

In the Old Testament, Daniel had an extraordinary spirit and was able to explain everyday enigmas:

> This was because an extraordinary spirit, knowledge and insight, interpretation of dreams, explanation of enigmas and solving of difficult problems were found in this Daniel, whom the king named Belteshazzar. Let Daniel now be summoned and he will declare the interpretation. (Daniel 5:12 NASV)

The main puzzle or enigma for people is that what we see and focus on is eventually what we believe. Figure 10.1 is a world-famous image of an illusion entitled *Enigma*, designed by Isia Leviant (1981), Palais de la Découverte, Paris. As you stare at the center circle you will eventually see the outer circles appear to rotate or the lines between the circles start to move.

If you did not see any movement in Figure 10.1, take a look at Figure 10.2, another picture in which pinwheels appear to be moving when combined with each other.

Figure 10.1: The Enigma Illusion

Figure 10.2: An Enigma Pinwheel

The purpose of these images within this spiritual bulletin is to illustrate the importance of taking into consideration what we are seeing and focusing our eyes and minds on. What we set our eyes on and start focusing on begins the process of determining what we envision and believe. What we start seeing and believing becomes so true in our eyes and minds that we can't see the real truth behind the thing. This is the very reason that Jesus asks the Pharisees, "What did you go out to see?" (Matthew 11:7–10) instead of "What did you go out to hear?" when they went out to hear John the Baptist. Jesus was less interested in what they heard than what they saw because He knows what we see will eventually be what we believe.

One of the main reasons so many people are unfocused and disillusioned in life is that the center of their views or reference points may not be the proper reference points. Below are a few examples of the wrong primary reference points.

+ If I put my marriage at the center of my sight, before long I start seeing or imagining things moving around my marriage, but in reality they are not actually moving.
+ If I put church at the center of my sight, before long I start seeing or imagining things moving around my church or pastor, but in reality they are not actually moving.
+ If I put my job/career at the center of my sight, before long I start seeing or imagining things moving around my job/career, but in reality they are not actually moving.
+ If I put myself at the center of my sight, before long I start seeing or imagining things moving around myself, but in reality they are not actually moving.

If you could step back and imagine placing noncritical views of life at the center of your sight, you may be able to imagine how your view could get distorted. Worse yet, if you multiplied the number of wrong critical views at the center of the pinwheel diagram in Figure 10.2, you would quickly start imagining that multiple things were moving when actually they were staying the same. This is why so many people get near the ends of their lives and realize not much has actually changed. We could state that this is the enigma of your life; how many things have really changed as opposed to what we thought changed? If we are honest we will admit God has given us the keys to the kingdom and we can lock and unlock the mysteries of our lives. This means that spiritual, emotional, mental, financial, and even physical things can be reversed and restored. Unfortunately, many people have set their primary sights on earthly things such as marriages, jobs, money, careers, retirement, bodies, health, and selves.

Let's take this discussion to the core of the matter: viewing the things of earth versus the things of heaven.

+ If I put a church denomination at the center of the pinwheels, before long everything in the kingdom of God starts moving around the denomination, as that is the center point.

- If I put the physical church building I attend at the center of the pinwheels, before long everything in the kingdom of God starts moving around the church, as that is the center point.
- If I put a minister at the center of the pinwheels of my life, before long everything in the kingdom of God starts moving around the minister, as he or she is the center point.
- If I put heavenly or kingdom things at the center of the pinwheels of my life, before long everything in the kingdom starts moving around my life and heavenly or kingdom things start happening in my life. This if course is the preferred method of living and why Jesus says to put the kingdom of God first in our lives.

These simple examples help reveal the importance of what Jesus said: "Seek you first the Kingdom of God and His righteousness and the rest of things would follow" (Matthew 6:33). When the kingdom of God is at the center of my focus, the other things I need will start moving around the center of my focus.

What is the Remedy for the Enigma Quandary?

If we follow scripture in its simplest form, we can determine what we should set our sights on, our reference point:

1. Be born again. Jesus told Nicodemus that he could never "see" the movement of the kingdom if he was not born again. (John 3:3)
2. "Seek you first the Kingdom of God and His righteousness and then all the other things will follow and be added unto you" (Matthew 6:33). We must put the kingdom first so all secondary things start revolving around it.
3. Set your affections on heavenly things versus earthly things: "Since, then, you have been raised with Christ, set your hearts on things above, where Christ is seated at the right

hand of God. Set your minds on things above, not on earthly things." (Colossians 3:1–2)

On one side of the enigma quandary my wife and I have taken many arrows of accusations stating that we are often too focused on heavenly things and that our expectations for heavenly things are set too high. We are pleased that after all these years our choice to put heavenly things and the kingdom of God in the center of our sights has paid huge dividends. It has also allowed us to see and experience the greater things that Jesus referenced.

On the other side of the enigma quandary I have seen people who placed their earthly and tangible needs, concerns, and ideas at the center of their sights and now reap the fruit of earthly things. I must say that heavenly things taste far better, last far longer, and bring God far greater credit and glory.

The enigma of our day is that people have set their center sights on things other than the kingdom of God and/or heavenly promises, and this is becoming very visible. Many people have put politics, religions, social churches, feel-good music, body paintings and piercings, ministers, spouses, jobs, careers, money, leisure, retirement, fitness, food, health, and other trends at the center of their visions and sights. Even though we can argue that most of these things are acceptable and even good in moderation, they cannot compete with the center of our lives being focused on God's kingdom and his righteousness.

One of the enigma scripture passages I used (Matthew 6:22–23), states that the light of the body is the eye, and if your eye is clear, your whole body should be full of light, but if your eye is full of darkness, your whole body will be full of darkness. This passage is preceded and followed by the admonishments that wherever your treasure is located, there will your heart be also. (Matthew 6:21, 24).

In many respects our eyes are windows into our bodies, minds, and souls, so it is critical that we be careful what we see and what we don't see. As you have gleaned from the images in Figures 10.1 and 10.2, when we focus on a center point, a reference point, our eyes and minds can see things that are only perceptions. This same concept applies in other images or walks of life. How did a gambler become a gambler, or how did an adulterer become an adulterer, or how did a thief become a thief, or how did an addict become an addict? How did a marriage end in divorce? How did a believer become an unbeliever? The answers to these questions are never simple, but in almost all cases the problems stared by visions being set on the wrong reference points. Below is a nice reminder of how important it is to watch what we set our sights on.

Watch your eyes and what reference points you set your sight upon.

Watch your sight, for it may become what you start focusing on.

Watch what you focus on, for it may be what you believe.

Watch what you believe, for it may become what you dwell upon.

Watch what you dwell upon, for it may be what or whom you serve.

Watch what and whom you serve, for it may become your destiny!

CHAPTER 11

THE PRINCIPLE OF THE MERCHANT AND PEARL

By Pamela Mathews

Again, the kingdom of heaven is like a merchant seeking for fine pearls!

—Matthew 13:25

Our deepest fear is not that we are inadequate. Our deepest fear is that we are powerful beyond measure. It is our light, not our darkness, that most frightens us. We ask ourselves, who am I to be brilliant, gorgeous, talented, and fabulous? Actually, who are you not to be? You are a child of God. You playing small does not serve the world. There's nothing enlightened about shrinking so that other people won't feel insecure around you. We are all meant to shine, as children do. We are born to make manifest the glory of God that is within us. It is not just in some of us, it's in everyone. And as we let our own light shine, we unconsciously give other people permission to do the same. As we are liberated from our own fear, our presence automatically liberates others.

—Marianne Williamson

The birth of a pearl is truly a miraculous event. Unlike gemstones or precious metals that must be mined from the earth, pearls are grown by oysters far below the surface of the sea. Gemstones must be cut and polished to bring out their beauty, but pearls need no such treatment to reveal their loveliness. They are born from oysters complete with a shimmering iridescence, luster, and soft inner glow unlike any gem on earth.

A natural pearl begins its life as a foreign object such as a parasite or piece of shell that accidentally lodges itself in an oyster's soft, inner body where it cannot be expelled. To ease this irritant the oyster's body takes defensive action by secreting "nacre," a smooth, hard, crystalline substance around the irritant to protect itself. As long as the irritant remains in its body, the oyster will continue to secrete nacre around it, layer upon layer. Over time the irritant will be completely encased by the silky, crystalline coatings, and the ultimate result is a lovely and lustrous pearl.

How something so wondrous emerges from an oyster's way of protecting itself is one of nature's loveliest surprises. The nacre, not just a soothing substance, is composed of microscopic crystals of calcium carbonate aligned perfectly with one another so that light passing along the axis of one crystal is reflected and refracted by another to produce a rainbow of light and color.

The Miraculous Birth of the Pearls of Your Past, Present, and Future

The full birth of whom God designed you to be is a miraculous event. God creates us in his image but with a fallen nature because of the fall of Adam and Eve. Along our lives' journeys many irritants such as disappointments, broken relationships, lack of self-worth, dysfunctional family traits, addictions, financial issues, thoughts of death, self-hatred, loss of hope, parasites, and many other clingy things collect in the closets of our lives. As our lives progress, the illusion of fear and failure combine to force us to escape or resent the memories of our pasts, which in turn affect our presents and eventually hinders our futures.

God has allowed you as an individual to review your collection of irritants in a manner that allows Him to shine light into your past, present, and future simultaneously. This review allows you to be thankful or exchange the irritants for a realignment that perfectly connects your past, present, and future via God's light. These light rays into your past, present, and future allow you to view the pearl of your life represented by a full rainbow of light and color that connects your past, present, and future into the miracle God always intended. Are you ready to begin the journey of finding the pearl within by exchanging the irritants of your life for the miracle God intended? Should you embark on this personal journey, you will be challenged to exchange your irritants for personal pearls.

The *Pearl Within Journey* includes various areas of your life that generally need to be refined, cultivated, and rid of irritants that have blocked the light rays of completeness to shine upon your pearl. If you have released or exchanged your irritants over time, the journey may be simple. However, if you have built up your irritants or hidden them through the years, the process could be lengthy and painful but every bit worth it as you begin seeing the pearls within you!

Many people seek for greater things such as greater meaning, greater understanding, greater wealth, greater relationships, greater significance, etc. The Bible is clear that we are to seek, ask, and knock (Matthew 7:7). In essence, the Bible encourages you to improve and become the person God created you to be. Taking this one step further, Jesus encourages you to not only believe in Him but to expect to do even greater works than He did (John 14:12). Last, God states that He has given you the keys to the kingdom of heaven so that you can bind and loosen things in your life, your family's life, and other people's lives.

Let it be known that for all who have allowed their pasts to block their futures, feel inadequate, feel failures, feel dysfunctional, feel incompetent, feel unworthy, feel relationally inept, God has given them the keys to start finding and unlocking the pearls within!

Without a doubt, God has designed us to become more than many of us have become. However, few people have realized the simple process in which this takes place; it can be explained in scripture by stating what the kingdom of heaven is truly like. Open your hearts, listen, and pray over the following scripture passage:

> Again, the kingdom of heaven is like a merchant looking for fine pearls. When he found one of great value, he went away and sold everything he had and bought it. (Matthew 13:45–46)

This passage is vital to understanding a simple process that many people overlook. In this passage the object of discovery is a pearl of great value, and the subject surrounding the object of great value is the kingdom of heaven. Jesus was instructing us that the kingdom of heaven is like a merchant who is looking for fine pearls and finally finds one of great value, and he is willing to exchange all else to get it. Therefore, the kingdom of God includes an exchange process as we progress through our asking, seeking, and knocking (Matthew 7:7). The doors of your opportunity begin to open and close with the key of exchange!

This passage is the key to your personal journey through the *Pearl Within Journal*. The kingdom of heaven and the keys God gave you to loosen and bind the issues within the kingdom are very similar to the journey of finding the great pearl within you. In order to recognize and obtain the great pearl you must exchange the issues of life. Simply put, the keys to the kingdom of God that allow you to loosen and bind (Matthew 16:19) are the very process of exchange.

This process is so simple that at first glance it may appear complicated. The great news is that throughout scripture and our everyday lives the process of exchange is shown as the key to getting the very things God intended for us. Below is a long list of exchanges that have taken place that have advanced the kingdom.

- God so love the world that He exchanged His one and only begotten Son so that we might believe and be saved.

- Jesus exchanged His blood and body for our eternal salvation when he was on the cross. He set the example of exchange for us to follow. This is why he commands us to also exchange by "taking up our cross daily."

+ Adam and Eve exchanged a life of perfection for a sinful future by eating of the tree of knowledge of good and evil.

+ Adam and Eve exchanged one more time by shedding the blood of an animal to cover up their newfound sin.

+ Noah exchanged the destruction of his family by having faith that rain would flood the earth even when there had never been any rain. He exchanged his role as a shepherd and shipbuilder for the title of a righteous preacher through his act of faith.

+ Jacob exchanged His name for Israel upon confession of who he really was.

+ Jonah exchanged his position in the belly of the whale when he committed to go to Nineveh.

+ Joshua exchanged his lack of hope for victory when he listened to the voice of God to get up from prayer and move into action.

+ Solomon exchanged his inexperience as a king with the greatest wisdom in the world by acting and believing in his dream.

+ Rahab, the prostitute, exchanged her faith for a place in the lineage of Jesus.

+ The Apostle Paul exchanged his position as a martyr of Christians by asking God what He wanted from his life when he fell off his horse on the way to Damascus.

+ Joseph and Mary exchanged their shame of having a child out of wedlock and became the parents of the greatest prophet and Messiah by believing what the angel of the Lord said to them.

+ The apostle John exchanged his fear of isolation and visions and wrote the greatest revelation of all time, the book of Revelation.

+ All sinners exchanged their lives of sin by confessing that Jesus died on the cross for their sinful life in order to become Christians.

+ Many people in the New Testament exchanged their faith for a healing; as God said, "Your faith has made you whole."

Simple and Personal Life Examples

+ I exchanged my single life for the married life. The things I used to do with my single friends were exchanged for activities with my spouse and family.

+ I exchanged marriage vows with my spouse, making a commitment to be devoted to my spouse until death.

+ I exchanged my feelings of a dysfunctional family by confessing that all families were born sinful and therefore dysfunctional.

+ I exchanged my college tuition for a college degree.

+ I exchanged my college degree for a job in the computer industry.

+ I exchanged my past failings with God's forgiveness by confessing those past failings. In exchange, God gave me a future direction.

+ I exchanged my love for alcohol with a love for God's Word once I realized I could ask for deliverance.

+ I exchanged some of my retirement funds for a loan for my daughter's education.

The process of exchange is what advanced the kingdom of God as well as my personal life. Old and New Testament people advanced the kingdom and unlocked doors by exchanging what they had for something better. This is why Jesus stated that we could have the keys to the kingdom of heaven to bind and loosen things on earth. Even though this is a limited list of exchanges, any of us would be hard pressed to find examples where things are advanced or improved without a form of exchange.

Consider the mere fact that Jesus was used as the ransom and sacrifice for my sins. Even though He paid the price through the sacrifice, three forms of exchange had to take place for the ransom or sacrifice to have meaning.

1. God had to exchange with humanity by giving His Son in an earthly form.

2. Jesus had to exchange His position, come to earth, and die a sacrificial death.

3. All sinners have to exchange by confessing that Jesus Christ died for their sins before the ransom or sacrifice is applied to them personally.

Even though we claim salvation is free, we need to admit that there is a price to be paid and that we cannot claim our salvations without exchanging with God our confessions that we were born sinners.

The simplicity of the process of exchange is best explained by understanding the simplicity of a relationship. In every living relationship there is a process of exchange; there is no healthy relationship where there is no ongoing exchange. This includes relationships with God, spouses, children, friends, family, and coworkers, but most of all with yourself. Note again that Jesus said that the kingdom of heaven is like a merchant of pearls who is willing to exchange all for the great pearl. Possibly Jesus used this parable to indicate that we must be like merchants, knowing that merchants are exchangers of goods. Merchants are also always asking, seeking, and knocking for greater goods to improve their positions. If we are commanded to continue to ask, seek, and knock, we should conclude that we are always finding and learning greater things we can exchange for. In fact, we can take all the irritants of our lives and exchange them for greater things. This is possible when God's light shines truth and revelation on my irritants, transforming them into the greatest pearl within me.

This process of exchange will be the basis for every chapter within the journal; the keys to your personal healing and the keys to the kingdom of heaven cannot be used without an exchange. Are you willing to exchange to see God's full light come into each area of your life to make your past, present, and future the full rainbow of perfect light, color, and reflection that God intended it to be? Your pearl within is waiting for the full light of God to be reflected!

If the key to finding your pearl within is the action of exchange, every chapter of this journal will require action on your part to exchange things from your past, present, and future to identify the fullness and completeness of the one God created you to become. Because God did not wake up today and change His mind about you or whom He created you to become, He desires you to ask, seek, knock as you exchange your entire past, present, and future ambitions. This process for the theological-at-heart would be known as the process of redemption. God instituted the process of redemption through many facets including covenants, testaments, and promises throughout scripture. However, the full nature of redemption does not reach full value and maturity until we meet Christ in heaven (Ephesians 1:14). This indicates that the exchange or redemptive process is an ongoing transaction. This is very much what God intended when He said, "And we, who with unveiled faces all reflect the Lord's glory, are being transformed into his likeness with ever-increasing glory, which comes from the Lord, who is the Spirit." (2 Corinthians 3:18)

Begin the process of ever-increasing glory in your life by allowing the opportunity and privilege to exchange whom you and others thought you were with whom God created you to be, as this is truly your pearl within!

It will excite you to learn that in Genesis 9:13–17 God made a covenant, an agreement of exchange, that he will use a cloud and a rainbow to remind Himself and us of His everlasting agreement of love for humanity. Rainbows created by light rays of reflection and refraction are a great reminder of God's light that is able to reflect and refract the beauty of whom he created you to be, beauty that can be found if you search and decide to exchange with Him.

CHAPTER 12

THE PRINCIPLE OF THANKSGIVING WORSHIP

By Pamela Mathews

In everything give thanks, for this is the will of God in Christ Jesus concerning you.

—1 Thessalonians 5:18

If anyone would tell you the shortest, surest way to happiness and all perfection, he must tell you to make it a rule to yourself to thank and praise God for everything that happens to you. For it is certain that whatever seeming calamity happens to you, if you thank and praise God for it, you turn it into a blessing.

—Unknown

In 2008, God allowed me to take thankfulness to a higher and more complete level. This transition has truly allowed me to see my pearl within. We mentioned that a pearl begins by being a simple irritant in an oyster that begins the process of many layers of cover-up to protect the oyster. In my life I had built up hundreds of irritants I decided to forget about, ignore, or in a few cases become bitter over.

Once my view of thankfulness changed, I saw the irritants of my life as things to be thankful for because they were the very things that made me who I am today. Without these irritants I would have been a very limited human being with lesser value. However, the great secret for me was to clean out this lack of thankfulness in my mind and my heart. I was not able to see my full value until I understood the complete healing power of thankfulness for all things. My room of thankfulness was swept, cleaned, and given a complete makeover.

Let me explain. As have many people, I always viewed myself as a thankful type of person because I was thankful for the good things I could embrace in my past, present, and future. My view of my past, present, and future was generally within a six- to twelve-month window of time. For instance, I was thankful for my children's grades, my husband's promotion, that we paid our bills last month, that my family was healthy, that we had found a good church, that we found a new house, that we were going on a family vacation, that we had a good pastor, that we saw God heal our daughter's sickness, that our minivan was repaired, that my parents were healthy, and so on. You get the idea! So during most of my life, if people were to ask me if I was thankful, I would say absolutely! This thankful lifestyle allowed me to progress through life in six- to twelve-month time frames and left me feeling somewhat happy and content.

This same process is possibly why the dreaded Christmas letter was invented. It is a great means to reflect on your thankfulness over the last twelve months while giving everyone an update on your family and a Christmas card at the same time. (Long live the dreaded Christmas letter!)

What changed my whole view of complete thankfulness in 2012 was a new understanding of being thankful over a longer view of my life as well as some of the perceived negative circumstances of my life. This recently found understanding was as if God's light and love shined a huge spotlight over specific negative circumstances of my past and healed them instantaneously. My life suddenly reflected something of greater value even though nothing had changed except my confession of thanksgiving over those secret, hidden, or forgotten circumstances I never thought possible to thank God for. I am still amazed at what God's light and love illuminated in me. The thought of giving thanks for these things years ago was just incomprehensible. Listen to the things that started to come out of my mouth once I understood the completeness of thanksgiving!

- Thank you that my husband was an alcoholic for the first five years of our marriage! This gave me an idea of what spouses of alcoholics go through.

- Thank you that I was insecure over many things in my life! This allowed me to be dependent on God and thirst after his righteousness.

- Thank you that I was stubborn over things that made no sense to be stubborn over; this helped me understand that fear and ignorance are the roots of stubbornness.

- Thank you I have dealt with such prideful people! It made me look at myself and realize I was a prideful person as well.

- Thank you that my children are not perfect! No one has perfect children, but they learn by their mistakes.

- Thank you my marriage was a mess for the first five years! I find that I am able to help women who are in similar circumstances. I found how dependent on God I really am for my marriage to work.

- Thank you for the disagreements in my relationships! This allowed me to see who people really are and love them unconditionally.

- Thank you that I lived in fear during the majority of my life!

I now realize that most people live in some type of fear and that only faith can conquer fear.

♦   Thank you for my mind's confusion that created periodic depression! It helped me expand my mind in proportion to my heart. God was looking for me to serve Him with all my heart and mind. I received a full cleansing of my heart and mind because of this struggle.

♦   Thank you for my financial ups and downs! I was able to look at the true meaning of wealth and not focus on money.

How did this new process of allowing God's light to reflect on my perceived issues come into being? I was listening to Mike speak to leaders who were discussing the topic of repenting over the past circumstances in a specific area of sin. One person stated that he did not think this group of leaders could progress until there was another attempt at repenting over the issues at hand. My husband quickly replied, "I do not believe God's desire is to have us keep repenting the same issues over and over." He felt that the group needed to release God's revelation into the situation. Within seconds there was a moving of God's presence that allowed one person after another to start thanking God for the issues of life that they had felt shameful of and had repented over numerous times already. Suddenly there was the most quick and powerful presence of God's Spirit I had felt in my life; it was as if people were giving God praise for the irritants in their lives even if they were negative experiences. What I witnessed was a supernatural healing of the things people had been covering up, hiding, or unable to get permanent healing for.

For the next year Mike preached and shared in numerous settings and allowed a new form of worship to take place by giving full thanks to God. I was part of this process in numerous settings, over and over witnessing people begin the process of thanking God for things they never knew they should or could be thankful for. Time and again most people stated that they felt a healing or release from the very thing that hindered their lives. These hundreds of people along with me experienced a supernatural exchange with God that set them free from years of hidden and shameful experiences. Metaphorically speaking, I witnessed people spitting into the face of their own shame and Satan's accusations and releasing issues that were irritants in their lives for years. The positive confessions of thanksgiving were open exchanges with God, whose light, love, and Spirit are so powerful that when the areas of hurt were exposed by confessions of thanks they were instantaneously healed. It was like a radiation treatment hitting a spot of cancer and making it vanish. Pearls within were being discovered!

The exchange process in this thanksgiving type of worship is a positive, spiritual confession that allows God to heal a person's past and make him or her complete. This is truly an exercise of healing, and exchange in which God shows His pure and complete redemptive nature for the following scenarios of past shamefulness:

1. For people who have been violated by abusers, offenders, and criminals, God is able to fulfill His scripture that states He will turn evil into good. This allows them to wipe away the bitterness, shame, guilt, and ugliness that comes from being violated by someone else. Upon open thanksgiving, God exchanges complete healing. It is simply a process of exchange that allows your words of confession and thanksgiving to exchange with His light to allow your pearls within to be seen and harvested!

2. For people who have personally made mistakes by having put themselves in harm's way or having committed a crime or trespass against God or themselves, God's light and love can allow them to be forgiven, redeemed, and healed from mistakes that bring guilt and shame. Once again, upon the simple confession of thanksgiving they exchange their pasts and make the irritant of shame or guilt become their personal pearls within.

3. For people who feel they were just unfortunate, born into the wrong family, or unfortunate enough to have had bad things happen to them, God is able to take those irritants and allow them to be healers to themselves and others in similar circumstances. He can do this by shining His light

upon the confession of thanksgiving. Their exchanges allow the irritants of unfortunate circumstances to become their personal pearls within.

What I experienced was a glorious exchange that could have been done only with my willingness to simply become thankful for the greatest irritants of my life. This exchange produced an understanding that helped me see my personal pearl within, and it gave me a fuller desire to see others experience their pearls within. I desired to live out what the Bible states in Psalm 34:1–3: "I will bless [give thanks] to the Lord at all times, His praise shall continually be in my mouth. My life [entire life] will boast in the Lord so that the humbled and afflicted will hear [my thanksgiving] and be glad. Come on, and magnify the Lord with me, and let's exalt his name together."

My sincerest desire is to get all you readers to stop believing any hint that God is cruel or planned a cruel life for you. I want you all to see God as He really is, and just because someone has violated you or you have self-destructed, this does not define your fate. Rather, your fate rests in your ability and willingness to reason with God and allow Him to use your afflictions and irritants to define and reveal the pearl within you. Will you choose to let His light, love, and Spirit shine on your irritants by exchanging words of thanksgiving to your creator? Listen below to what John Henry Jowett penned as well as King David in the Book of Psalms.

> Being thankful over my entire past and future spits in Fear's face! Life without thankfulness is devoid of love and passion. Hope without thankfulness is lacking in fine perception. Faith without thankfulness lacks strength and fortitude. Every virtue divorced from thankfulness is maimed and limps along the spiritual road.
> —John Henry Jowett

> You turned my wailing into dancing; you removed my sackcloth and clothed me with joy, that my heart may sing to you and not be silent. O LORD my God, I will give you thanks forever. (Psalm 30:11, 12)

It was good for me to suffer, so that I might learn your statutes. (Psalm 119:71)

You can quickly surmise by these three examples that there is an exchange taking place when we openly confess that God has a reason, season, and purpose for our circumstances. If you cannot embrace this simple kind of faith, please know that His Light can zap your past issues and that He can redeem and exchange the issues. Your task is to consider your willingness to let faith move you toward God's greatness or let fear continue to hide your past shame, failings, and violations by others.

I was amazed to learn that the great football player Reggie White had a dream the week before he died on December 26, 2004. He told his wife, Sarah, that in his dream he saw two Hebrew words and understood them to be a great treasure. Upon prayer, meditation, and researching the two Hebrew words, he found that the treasure was the words' meaning, "Jehovah Redeems." Reggie found a treasure within himself before he died and shared it with others. This treasure is no different than the pearl within you. Jehovah redeems or exchanges with all who will reason out their options with Him. Upon giving God thanks, He is quick to redeem or exchange your issues to make you see your complete image inside of you.

I realize this concept of being thankful for everything is a stretch for many people. I know it took me months to grab hold of this concept in its fullest sense. I started stumbling for words, wrestling with whose fault it was, wondering if I could forgive those who had wronged me. However, I was amazed that upon opening my mouth a sense of instant healing and cleansing came. I believe it was an act of faith to move my lips, and upon spilling out the words of confusion God became my judge, the righteous judge working on my behalf who did what He does best: redeem and exchange the confession. I think this is the very act that God mentions in Ecclesiastes 12:14: "For God will evaluate every deed, including every secret thing, whether good or evil." God will eventually evaluate or judge everything in secret or in open to determine whether it was good or evil. My confession gives me credit to let him evaluate or judge this in my present life. I do not want it hidden, as I desire full redemption for my sins and other people who sinned against me.

Even if I sin and cause problems, God encourages me to be willing to discuss this with him and be forgiven of everything. However, if I choose not to openly discuss matters with God, I may find that the things I hide will devour me like a sword. This is the context of Isaiah 1:17–19. I am so glad God gave options for every scenario of life whether I am guilty or someone else is. This is the very reason Jesus was able to ask God to forgive those who violated His position, status, knowledge, name, body, and blood. I have not known this type of violation in my past. However, it gives me a reference point as to how far I can go and still give God thanks and have enough faith to ask Him to forgive the vilest of offenders and offenses against me.

Now that you have read my story of finding the pearl within me through complete thanksgiving, let us do a few exercises in our *Pearl Within Journal.* Some of these exercises may need to be revisited, as your ability for being free of your past and truly thanking God for all things may not occur until a few more journeys in the journal are complete.

As you have read my story of raising my thanksgiving to a new level, I am sure that you have been processing your own thoughts as to the possibility for you to be thankful for past experiences.

Please do not give up on processing the thanksgiving aspect. If you have a few circumstances that are too overwhelming to deal with right now, we can park those for the time being. I understand the difficulty of being thankful for very stressful, traumatic, and painful experiences. In some cases, before you can thank God you have to forgive yourself or the person who violated you. Because this is so critical, I have created table 12.1 as a parking space for these types of circumstances that will allow you to "park" any extremely painful or unforgiven circumstances for the time being and allow you to move forward with thanksgiving in most other areas.

No.	Items too Difficult to Thank God about at the Present Time
1.	

No.	Items too Difficult to Thank God about at the Present Time
2.	
3.	
4.	

Table 12.1: Parking Space for Circumstances That Are too Difficult

Table 12.2 is a checklist that may help you identify levels of thanksgiving. The column on the left includes samples of standard items that are easy to be thankful for. The column on the right includes samples of items much more difficult to be immediately thankful about.

Standard, Easy Circumstances	More Difficult Circumstances
Good health	A bad health experience
An afflicted person who gets healed	An afflicted person who dies
A stable job or career	A recent job or career change that seemed unpleasant
A mortgage-free house	Loss of house through foreclosure, tornado, hurricane, etc.
Children's health and success	Children who are challenging
The perfect and loving family that prays together, stays together, etc. (you know the cliché)	Dysfunctional family (alcoholic parent[s], addictive and abusive behavior patterns, financial distress, etc.)
Wealth or financial freedom	Financially dependent on others
Parents who are still married	Divorced parents, parents in prison, adopted, or removed from home by the state
Good church	Shunned by church or don't fit in

Standard, Easy Circumstances	More Difficult Circumstances
Natural ability or talented in a specific area	Everything comes hard and unnatural—must work extra hard for everything you get
Complete family is saved and in perfect health	Son or daughter was murdered, died in a war, died at birth, car accident, drug overdose, child raped or kidnapped, etc.
Periods of time where everything turns to gold	Periods of time where everything turns to rust or bust
Supportive spouse	Abusive spouse
A great marriage that thrives	A marriage always threatened by divorce
Married	Divorced
Faithful spouse	Affair committed by spouse
Lots of friends	Loss of close friends
Sexually unscathed and pure	Sexually immoral or raped
Desirable in church because of knowledge or talent	Undesirable in church
Success with projects at work	Failure with projects at work
Great boss	Demanding and difficult boss
Blank Spaces Are for Your Personal Examples	

Standard, Easy Circumstances	More Difficult Circumstances

Table 12.2 – List of things to be thankful about

If you are able to thank God for all the events or circumstances in the left column, you are like most people who find it easy to thank God when things are going well. However, a truly thankful person is able to look at even unfortunate circumstances and reason with God on why they happened. Through the reasoning process they learn that God ultimately is pleased when we thank him for going through afflictions so that we are better people. Notice I did not say thank Him for the afflictions, but thank Him for allowing you to make it through the afflictions to be a better person.

Challenge Question

To error is human; to blame others is even more human. Reflect on the last year and estimate how much time you invested in either being suspicious that someone hurt you or how much you have been hurt versus how much time you gave negative circumstances over to God to heal and wipe the hurt out of your mind.

1. Time estimate on how much time was invested on suspicion and/or hurt: _____ hours

2. Time estimate on how much time was invested in giving issue to God: _____ hours

God knows as well as most mature people do that where there are no shipwrecks there are no lighthouses. Some of my personal shipwrecks have produced great lighthouses in my life. Mike and I have a friend who had three marriages, and each of his wives left on bitter terms. Through his struggles he became a minister to an area that experiences a high rate of divorce. He became a lighthouse because of his affliction. Another friend, Clay McClary, whose son was murdered, spent eight years tracking down the murderer to kill him. After the eighth year, God told Clay that he must forgive his son's murderer. Through the affliction Clay went on to be a minister of the Gospel and give his testimony of exchanging anger for love. Clay was another shipwreck who learned to thank God for the experience. Without thanking God, he could not have become the person God desired him to be. The full testimony of Clay McClary is at: http://www.focusonheaven.com/redemptioncenter.html.

You have been challenged to think about a new level of thankfulness. Now we are ready to embark on an actual exercise to allow you the opportunity to exchange with God on a personal level. Pick out three positive and three negative experiences you have experienced in your life. Spend three minutes thanking God verbally for the positive circumstances. Now spend three minutes thanking God for the negative circumstances. Write your three positive and negative circumstances in Table 12.3 so you can focus on how you might say a prayer of thanksgiving for negative circumstances. I have added a third column, "Reasons why the negative experiences ended up being valuable," to help you verbalize in your prayer of thanksgiving how you might be thankful you made it through the negative circumstances.

Thanking God for Three Positive Circumstances	Thanking God for Three Negative Circumstances	Reasons Why the Negative Circumstances Ended Up Being Valuable
1.	1.	1.
2.	2.	2.
3.	3	3.

Table 12.3 – Thankful experiences

Please record how you felt after spending three minutes on three of your negative circumstances. Also, record how hard it was to focus three minutes on negative circumstances.

Record How you felt before, during and after the prayer:

_____

_____

_____

_____

What you are experiencing may feel awkward, but the awkwardness will have tremendous payback if you follow through. Many of the rooms in our hearts such as bitterness, unforgiveness, anger, sexuality, and control are directly related to our ability to thank God for the circumstance from the past. Failure to deal with the past produces the clutter by not exchanging the issues of life with God's redemptive power.

Recall that the altar in its simplest form is the place where we met God to exchange our earthly issues for heavenly elements. Giving thanks for all things may be the exercise that allows us to experience God's full, redeeming nature. If all we did was thank God for positive things, there would be no need for exchange or redemption. The greatness of God comes when we have severe issues that need to be exchanged. Perhaps God sees our willingness to thank Him as an extraordinary act of faith that allows a complete healing of the past.

In the Old Testament (Genesis 37–43), Joseph suffered during his life a great number of afflictions and sufferings:

+ being sold by his brothers
+ being left for dead by his brothers
+ being accused of rape
+ being falsely imprisoned
+ being removed from his family for many years

In spite of all these afflictions, Joseph decided to name his first son Manasseh, which means "God says he has made me forget all my toil and all my father's house." He named his second child Ephraim, which means "God has made me to be fruitful in the land of my affliction." Somehow Joseph understood that without his many afflictions he would not have benefited later in life. He felt so strongly about giving God thanks for his afflictions and sufferings that he named his second child as a memory of this true concept in his life. Joseph learned the process and value of exchanging with God.

Let me close by sharing the very scripture that helps explain: "Give thanks in all circumstances, for this is God's will for you in Christ Jesus" (1 Thessalonians 5:18). This passage tells us that in all circumstances we are to give thanks, for this is God's will for us! God did not say to give thanks only in positive circumstances, for anyone can do that. The truly faithful learn to let their pasts heal their futures, as Joseph did. "The second son he named Ephraim and said, 'It is because God has made me fruitful in the land of my suffering'" (Genesis 41.52). What personal afflictions similar to Joseph's life have you experienced? And have you given God thanks through some type of memorial or confession, as Joseph did?

CHAPTER 13

THE PRINCIPLE OF CLOUDS: KEEPING YOUR HEAD IN THE CLOUDS

He lays the beams of his chambers on the waters; he makes the clouds his chariot; he rides on the wings of the wind.
—Psalm 104:3

Clouds are used to protect, shade, shower, and shadow us on earth; and to shadow and reflect the promises between heaven and earth.

—Michael L. Mathews

There are hundreds of biblical references to clouds and the importance of clouds. As a teaser, below are three key scriptural aspects about clouds that may just get your head in the clouds.

1. God made a covenant with Noah referencing clouds and the rainbow:

    Whenever I bring clouds over the earth and the rainbow appears in the clouds, I will remember my covenant between me and you and all living creatures of every kind. Never again will the waters become a flood to destroy all life." (Deuteronomy 9:14)

2. God states that the clouds are his chariot and how he travels:

    Sing to God, sing praise to his name, extol him who rides on the clouds—his name is the LORD—and rejoice before him." (Psalm 68:4)

    He lays the beams of his upper chambers on their waters. He makes the clouds his chariot and rides on the wings of the wind. (Psalm 104.3)

3. Those who have accepted Christ will meet Him in the clouds:

    Look, he is coming with the clouds, and every eye will see him, even those who pierced him; and all the peoples of the earth will mourn because of him. So shall it be! Amen. (Revelation 1:17)

The above concepts are joined by the many other aspects of clouds that indicate God has used clouds for many reasons. Below are these additional aspects:

+   God gave Moses the Ten Commandments in the cloud on Mt. Sinai. (Exodus 24:16)

- ✦ God used a cloud to guide the Israelites out of Egypt. (Numbers 9:21)
- ✦ God spoke out of a cloud when Jesus was baptized to say, "This is my Son, in whom I am well pleased." (Mark 9:7)
- ✦ The transfiguration happened in a cloud. (Luke 9:34)
- ✦ Angels were robed in a cloud. (Revelation 10:1)
- ✦ The Israelites were baptized in the cloud. (1 Corinthians 10:2)
- ✦ Jesus ascended in a cloud. (Acts 1:9)

Reflections in the Clouds

One morning, during a flight to Chicago, my plane took a sharp turn away from the rising sun. As I was sitting on the left side of the plane I noticed how the clouds reflected the shadow of the airplane across the sky. Within just a second the plane's shadow shot across the entire sky as far as my eye could see. Up until this point I had never known that the combination of the sun and clouds could cause a full reflection across the sky.

This experience made me broaden my thoughts toward how we might meet the Lord in the sky. I imagined that Christ could be in one location and the brightness of the Lord would cause His image to be displayed across the entire sky. No matter where people would be on the clouds, they would see His image reflected across the sky and land on the Mount of Olives. In addition, it may happen on a morning when the clouds came down to earth where we would or could be caught up in meeting the Lord in the clouds, just as the Bible states. My imagination allowed me to realize that the clouds are versatile enough to allow Christ to appear and to allow us to be caught up with Him in a variety of ways.

Clouds Are Very Versatile

On February 26–27, 2010 the 650 residents of the small town of Lajamanu, Australia, witnessed hundreds of perch fall from the clouds. Some of the fish were alive and some were dead as they fell during the two-day period. Scientists say that this type of activity is not unheard of, and they assumed that a whirlwind or tornado had picked up the fish from a river or the sea and placed them in a freezing cloud. When fish get tossed or sucked inside clouds they may freeze and eventually drop down after traveling hundreds or thousands of miles. The story can be read and verified at:

http://blogs.abcnews.com/theworldnewser/2010/03/its-raining-fish-hallelujah-.html

I am sure most of you will want to verify this story as true. Below is a list of similar incidents.

- 1st century: Pliny the Elder wrote about storms of frogs and fish, foreshadowing many modern incidents.
- 1794: French soldiers stationed in Lalain, near Lille, reported toads falling from the sky during heavy rain.
- 1857: Sugar crystals as big as a quarter of an inch in diameter fell over the course of two days in Lake County, California.
- 1876: A woman in Kentucky reported meat flakes raining from the sky. Tests found the meat was venison.
- 1902: Dust whipped up in Illinois caused muddy rain to fall over many northeastern states.
- 1940: A tornado in Russia brought a shower of sixteenth century coins.
- 1969: Golf balls fell from the sky in Punta Gorda, Florida.
- 1976: Blackbirds and pigeons rained from the sky for two days in San Luis Obispo.

Biblical Analogy of Raining down Manna and Quail

If you read Exodus chapters 14–15 you will find that what happened to the Israelites as they were leaving Egypt may have included very similar activity. The story starts out with the Lord creating a strong east wind that parted the Red Sea (Exodus 14:21). Some translations say that the wind lasted all night in order to get all the Israelites across. It is possible that the strong wind scooped up many objects, including animals, fish, etc. An important observation is that just prior to the strong wind causing the sea to divide, God put a cloud in front and behind the Israelites (Exodus 14:19). The clouds would have easily held whatever was blown up from the sea.

A unique feature of clouds is that many have ice crystals capable of freezing whatever enters the cloud, so the clouds could have acted as refrigerators for whatever was blown up from the sea and dispensed as the Israelites needed food.

Oddly enough, the Lord led the Israelites by a cloud by day and a pillar of fire by night. Immediately following the Red Sea crossing by the Israelites, the Lord began to provide daily manna from heaven and quail that miraculously appeared on the ground (Exodus 15). The cloud that led them on their journey may have very well been the cloud that was at the Red Sea collecting the provision that was needed. It would have been a true O'Manna plan devised by the same God who travels on the clouds as His chariots.

Taking the recent story of perch raining down in Lajamanu, Australia, you can possibly see the miracle that God brought was indeed a miracle. At the same time, could it be that God wants us to start looking upward toward the clouds because our redemption is drawing closer and closer and He is coming in the clouds? (Revelation 1:17).

Scripture refers to the clouds as God's chariot, and He promises to send Jesus to meet us in the clouds. What an exciting day to start imagining what might be happening in the clouds. I think I might start putting my head in the clouds! I also might start looking upward not only for my redemption (Luke 21:28) but for my provision in these difficult times.

Our Great Cloud of Witnesses—
Personal Encounters of the Heavenly Kind

If you are paying attention to what is transpiring in many circles, there is a clear sign of the increase in people dying and going to be with the Lord, more people experiencing out-of-body experiences or visits to heaven through temporary death or visions, and more people having dreams about heaven.

The exciting aspect of this increase is that there appears to be more and more excitement about heaven and less fear of death. This also shows that a spiritual maturity is occurring as people are eagerly focused on the things above the earth rather than just on temporal life (Colossians 3:1–2).

The reason I am so excited is that I have seen personal visions, heard from others, and read in scripture that we not only have a cloud of witnesses that include the great people of the Bible, but our great cloud of witnesses includes our contemporaries, our families, friends, relatives, and great ministers who we know are in heaven being "witnesses on our behalf." Hebrews 12:1–2 states "Seeing we are encompassed about with such a great cloud of witnesses let us set aside every weight and sin that so easily besets us and run with patience the race that is set before us."

Our Great Cloud of Witnesses Include Our Contemporaries

Hebrews 12:1–2 describes the great cloud of witnesses that encompasses us. The word "great" in this context means "a multitude" or "many." We should assume it goes beyond the few hundreds of Old and New Testament saints to include everyone who is with Jesus and the Father in heaven. It includes my grandparents and friends who saw my potential and are now interceding, laughing, and cheering me on from heaven. In fact, Pam and I often think of Gene Rolland and Clayton McClary, two dear friends who went to heaven in the last few years. They were dedicated soul winners for the kingdom and viewed Pam and me as partners in soul winning. Since they have died and are now part of our great and personal cloud of witnesses, we have noticed an increase in our love and God-given ability to heal and win souls into the kingdom. On numerous occasions we have laughed as we said, "We can see Clayton laughing at us from the throne room as we heal another person or see another person saved."

Clayton was my personal friend and witness on earth who, as a seventy-year-old elder, said, "Mike, one day, all your dreams and desires for the kingdom will come to pass." In the last few years, as we have seen our dreams being fulfilled, we are reminded that our cloud of witnesses is very personal. We start to envision and believe that our friends and relatives are witnessing for us before the throne. We see them personally asking God to use two ordinary people, us. We also imagine them cheering us on because they personally know our struggles and challenges on earth.

I should mention the word "encompass" used in Hebrews 12:1–2 means "to surround" and represents a form of completeness. In other words, the great cloud of witnesses surrounds us to provide a sense of completeness in our calling.

Recent Examples of Deaths and Visions of Heaven

About six months ago I visited with a wise and godly businessman from Minnesota. He had informed me he had been led by dreams, visions, and prayers since he was thirteen, and he was then forty-eight. This successful businessman who had learned to practice the invisible aspects of the fullness of Christ (Colossians 1:15–16) immediately had my attention. This was very refreshing, as I normally have to persuade people to believe in God's dreams and visions. He shared a vision that he, his wife, and seven others witnessed in the evening sky over their home during 2009. The vision included an elderly woman, a child, and angels who were rejoicing. The elderly woman in the sky resembled one of their parents, and the child resembled a child of theirs who had gone home to be with the Lord at a very young age. The elderly lady picked up the boy and twirled the child in a joyful manner. As he was describing the vision he and others had witnessed, God began to speak to my Spirit to the reason and purpose of the vision. He continued to share that during the vision his wife went into the house to get a CD player and started playing music as the vision was transpiring in the sky over a few hours. They realized that the angels and elderly lady were all dancing to the very tunes of the music they were playing on their CD player. I could barely hold back what I was witnessing in my spirit and blurted out what I believed to be the interpretation of the vision they had.

My interpretation was that the personal vision was given to them to show that they had their own personal cloud of witnesses made up of their contemporaries, very personal, and literally in tune with what they were doing on earth. The businessman and I laughed and rejoiced over the simple yet broadening understanding of the great cloud of witnesses that surrounds us.

As each year passes, more people have had out-of-body experiences as well as dreams or visions of heaven. In almost all cases the people who have had out-of-body experiences of heaven make statements such as "Now that I have seen heaven, there is nothing that interests me but heaven." Assuming these encounters of the heavenly kinds are true, we could say that these people have also become witnesses to what is happening in heaven, thus part of the great cloud of witnesses surrounding us. I guess this may be what God mentions in 2 Corinthians 2:9 when He says, "Eye hath not seen nor ear heard the great things that God has prepared for those who love him."

The most recent story of two people dying in the same time period is that of Oral Roberts and one of his spiritual sons, Pastor Billy Joe Daugherty. These two men were from different generations but collectively witnessed millions of souls saved and healed on earth.

Upon their recent deaths, one expected and the other unexpected, was the realization that these two men will become part of the great cloud of witnesses in heaven and have the potential influence to shake the heavens and the earth with wisdom, love, and compassion from a heavenly viewpoint. I sense that God has begun orchestrating the grand finale and is bringing home those who will impact heaven in a reverse manner. We have all heard of terms such as reverse mortgages, reverse engineering, reverse education, etc. What if we could imagine that God is far more advanced than humanity and has created a reverse-salvation plan that now allows the great men, women, and children of earth to work side by side with the Master of redemption!

One of my personal heroes, Reggie White, died at the early age of forty-three, but the week before he died he had a dream of two Hebrew words that translated into "Jehovah redeems." Prior to that dream, Reggie had prayed that his life would be a living sacrifice even unto death. I would not be surprised if God has pulled Reggie into the greatest reverse-salvation plan of all time, directly from the throne room down toward earth. This would explain what Isaiah saw when he said that salvation will spring forth from the ground after heaven rains down. "You heavens above, rain down righteousness; let the clouds shower it down. Let the earth open wide, let salvation spring up, let righteousness grow with it; I, the LORD, have created it." (Isaiah 45:8).

Starting to Win Against our Accusers

In 2011, as God was revealing fresh ideas about the great cloud of witnesses, He allowed me to understand and see a visual tug of war. On one side of the rope were all my accusers through the years who found fault with, accused, doubted, and verbally assaulted my actions, character, and intents. This is the side of people who Satan uses as the accusers of the brethren to say, "Lord, don't you see what these people are saying about Mike?"

On the other side of the rope, which was suddenly winning the tug of war, God showed me family members, friends, relatives, and coministers who had died and were greater in number than my accusers. This side stands before His throne and wins the battle against my accusers. They are cheering me on, laughing, and making statements that may sound something like "Lord, forgive Mike's mistakes, and view his intent as we now do, and use him to a greater degree." In God's court of law or court of this tug of war, the Great Judge is hearing the truth about people like you and me. We are starting to feel more confident, assured, and aware that our contemporaries who are a part of our great cloud of witnesses are working for us. This great cloud of witnesses continues to grow, to surround us, and to encompass us as we realize we can now easily set aside the weights and sins of the accusers who have distracted us for years. This tug of war was truly a fresh and revealing look at Hebrews 12:1–2.

Are you ready, willing, and able to see the spiritual insight into your cloud of witnesses, which include your contemporaries who know your challenges, your purest motives, and desires? If you will open your spiritual eyes, the light of life will reflect truth and revelation off the retina of your spiritual eyes, and you may begin to see your fullest and surest calling. This is what is revealed in Ephesians 1:18: "I pray also that the eyes of your heart may be enlightened in order that you may know the hope to which he has called you, the riches of his glorious inheritance in the saints."

It's time we all open our spiritual eyes to see, hear, and appreciate the great cloud of witnesses God has gathered for us. Rejoice as your loved ones go home to be with the Lord and enter your side of the tug of war. Rejoice when some of the greatest ministers go home to be with the Lord and can now see salvation from a reversed aspect.

CHAPTER 14

FEARFULLY AND WONDERFULLY MADE

A Mandate for Faith

*Listen to me, you islands; hear this, you distant nations:
Before I was born the LORD called me; from my birth he
has made mention of my name.*

—Isaiah 49:1

*The faster we move in time via speed, thoughts, or
dreams—the more of the impossible or heavenly potential
we are able to experience.*

—Michael L. Mathews

I was driving down the road in a large motor home during some very violent winds on Interstate 44 between Springfield, Missouri, and Tulsa, Oklahoma. The motor home was rocking back and forth, and I heard a loud banging on its outside. With the wind and the semis racing past me that were creating even more wind, it was impossible to pull over. I decided to slow down and pull off the road at the next exit to see what the slamming noise was. I took the first exit and parked at an abandoned gas station. I got out and noticed one of the lower compartment doors was missing. I immediately felt sick to my stomach as I knew that the door would have caused a lot of damage if it had hit another vehicle on the highway because it was about two feet high and three feet wide and weighed about forty pounds.

I looked up toward the highway and noticed a van coming toward me, and within seconds it was right in front of me. The driver slammed on his brakes and jumped out of his vehicle. The next few seconds seemed to last a lifetime. The man getting out was about six feet seven and was moving aggressively toward the side of his van. He opened the side door and quickly brought out my motor home door and walked directly at me as if ready to wrap it around my neck.

My worst fears reached my brain within seconds as I started contemplating how I was going to handle this angry man, who I naturally assumed had been hit by my missing door. The man stepped up to me, using my door like a shield, and shouted in the wind, "Is this your door?" Like George Washington, I knew I could not tell a lie, especially since I was the only motor home on the road with a missing door. The man slammed down the door and said in a gentle voice, "I saw your door drop off back on the highway exit, and I thought I would do you a favor and pick it up for you."

I was in complete shock as I had been fearfully imagining the worst possible scenario was about to happen right there on the side of the road in an abandoned gas station. I sheepishly said "Yes, that happens to be my door. Thanks for picking it up." He smiled and got back in his van and aggressively drove off.

I breathed a huge sigh of relief and thanked God that my door experience was not nearly as bad as I had imagined it was going to be. I was amazed at the amount of thoughts that had raced through my mind in just a few short seconds. I had visual images ranging from being beaten to death on the side of the road to trying to find my tire iron to protect myself from this man racing toward me. I had even wondered for a brief second how Pam would react when she found me lying dead next to the motor home at an abandoned gas station. I even squeezed in a thought about the life insurance policy as I recalled a few recent TV shows where people were killed due to road rage. Like I said, those few seconds lasted a lifetime.

This experience reminded me why we as humans fear the worst-case scenario in almost all situations. Look over the list below and see if any of these scenarios fit you.

+ You are driving down the road and a police car is merely taking the same path as you. You immediately start to slow down with your heart beating faster than it was a few seconds earlier. You naturally assume they are looking to pull you over.

+ You get home and see a letter with an Internal Revenue Service return address. You immediately do a brain scan of your past years of tax activities and imagine a few reasons why the IRS may be after you only to find out it is an innocent statement from your state income tax return.

+ You are out eating with the family and you see a coworker eating lunch with a person of the opposite sex. You immediately imagine that the person is having an affair only to find out it is a relative who happened to be visiting.

+ Your children leave you a voicemail or text you asking to talk with you later in the day. As the day goes by you start imagining all the things that they will ask for or the possible bad news they will deliver. Later on, you find out that they only had a simple question.

+ Your boss calls and says that he/she needs to speak to you the first thing in the morning. During the night and morning you start imagining the possible trouble you may be in or the bad news they have to share. During the meeting you find out the boss wanted only to ask a simple and innocent question.

We could bring up a lot more scenarios that cause us to immediately think, fear, or dwell on the worst possible outcomes in our day-to-day circumstances. As humans, we are prone to immediately think of the negative and worst-case scenarios. This natural tendency or behavior is caused by the amygdala (ah mig dah lah) portion of our brains that is programmed to put us in survival mode. What this means is that no matter what circumstance we come into, our most basic brain function is to survive. This also means we are trained to have a primitive reflex to either fight or flee from situations we perceive as threats. During my motor home experience I immediately contemplated fighting my perceived enemy or taking flight through a lie or excuse why my door had flown into his van (even though that never happened).

The Base and Natural Part of Our Brain—the Amygdala

The word "amygdala" comes from the Greek word for almond. The amygdala, which is about the size and shape of an almond, sits in the brain's medial temporal lobe (the base), a few inches from either ear. All research points to the amygdala as the portion of the brain that creates fear, emotion, and the natural instinct for survival and reproduction. All the scenarios that were described above are reactions of the amygdala, which is so close to our ears that we can almost hear the whispers of fear when any uncertain circumstance or possible change comes into our brain.

Many modern-day thought leaders have labeled the function of amygdala the "lizard brain" effect, as a lizard is a type of survival animal that will fight or flee from circumstances. The ability to understand the amygdala is critical to help us overcome our natural tendencies to fear the worst, run from problems, and take flight when things don't go our way. The natural function of the amygdala hinders our doing the things we ought to do in order to see the greater aspects of the kingdom of God and heavenly things. Anything that requires stepping into the unknown or requires changes immediately kicks in this natural tendency. As with most things in life, the experience caused by the amygdala is worse for some people than others.

The modern-day business leader, speaker, author, and thought leader Seth Godin is renowned for his work in helping people overcome the lizard brain effect. His thoughts are that the lizard brain is the hindrance to why so many people shut down new ideas, avoid confrontation, or decide to fight their way out of circumstances. Without dealing with this natural part of our brain we are prone to always let fear drive our initial responses, actions, and behaviors. The concept can be seen in many of the meetings we have all sat in where a new idea comes to the forefront and the majority of instant thoughts revolve around fear and failure and are followed by famous one-liners:

+ Yeah but!
+ We have never done it that way before!
+ What if it doesn't work?
+ Shouldn't we let someone else try it first?
+ Let's form another committee to study the effect!
+ We can't afford anything new or different this year!

Remember that the little, almond-shaped amygdala sits within one inch of our ears and whispers these fearful reactions to us. A simple overview of the amygdala can be viewed at http://youtu.be/JAoFPIHBu6U.

Seth Godin, who has done humanity a huge favor by speaking, articulating, and writing on the fear factors that are natural for all people, wrote *Lynchpin*, a book that does much to help people identify the issue and come up with ways to minimize the effects of lizard brain. It is my opinion that God created the brain to naturally function in this manner to bring about the need for human interaction with God. Even though the amygdala portion of our brain creates fear, another portion knows enough to operate in faith. When we mature and exercise faith, we are naturally bringing God into our circumstances to help us overcome our natural tendencies to depend merely on ourselves.

This concept and balance is more than likely what David had in mind when he said, "I praise you because I am fearfully and wonderfully made;

your works are wonderful, I know that full well" (Psalm 139:14). David knew he was driven by fear, and yet God made a wonderful way to seek help and find a balance between being fearful and yet wonderfully made.

A Biblical Perspective—The Mandate for Faith

God has done mankind a wonderful favor by designing our brains with this base function of being driven by fear. The reason this is such a huge favor is that it allows God to prove that mankind is limited in its ability to step up to a higher level of action, belief, hope, and destiny without acting by faith. As much as we want to rule over this human survival-or-fear effect, we must exercise faith to move past our human mechanisms. Humankind is very limited to the kingdom of God without interacting by faith in God's kingdom. This is why Hebrews 11:6 says, "Without faith it is impossible to please God." Fear causes people to remain creatures of habit (survival), while faith drives people to act in the realm of the unknown. In other words, the things we want to do we cannot do within ourselves. This is exactly what the Apostle Paul states in Romans 7:15–19 when he says he really doesn't understand himself because that which he wants to do he does not do, and that which he hates to do he actually does. The Apostle Paul more than likely did not know about the amygdala part of the brain, but he clearly understood that our human nature does not want to do the things that require faith and grace.

> I don't really understand myself, for I want to do what is right, but I don't do it. Instead, I do what I hate. And if I do what I do not want to do, I agree that the law is good. I know that nothing good lives in me, that is, in my sinful nature. For I have the desire to do what is good, but I cannot carry it out! For what I do is not the good I want to do; no, the evil I do not want to do—this I keep on doing. (Romans 7:15–19)

God has done all things well by creating our brains to protect us from doing harmful things that risk our survival yet allow us to exercise faith to accomplish things beyond our capability. This is why the Apostle Paul does not call it quits when he recognizes that he does the very things he knows he does not want to do. He makes a statement of faith in Galatians 2:20: "The life I live in the body, I live by faith in the Son of God, who loved me and gave himself for me." Paul realized that faith bridges our human frailty and moves us into heavenly realms of blessing, favor, and authority. We will never do the things of God, see the things of God, and act on behalf of the things of God with just our own human mechanisms. Simply put, we need God to balance our fear mechanisms!

Even though Jesus knew the human brain was meant to protect us for the purpose of survival, He also knew that faith in Him would allow us to be able to rule over this human fear. He knew in advance that faith is the victory that overcomes human and worldly fears. I appreciate Seth Godin's ability to help minimize all the negative people we naturally deal with, but God's solution of faith is ultimately the better answer and solution.

> For everyone born of God overcomes the world. This is the victory
> that has overcome the world, even our faith. (1 John 5:4)

This concept of human fear versus godly faith is of utmost importance because faith and fear are in opposition to one another. The more fear I have, the less faith I have; the more faith I have, the less fear I have. Jesus warned that in the last days of this world one of the epidemics of our time would be that people's hearts would fail them due to increasing amounts of fear (Luke 21:16). God knew ahead of time that the increase in information, knowledge, and decisions would make our amygdala work in overdrive, almost on a 24/7 basis. The stress at this increased level would cause an enormous amount of anxiety, fear, anger, resentment, and depression. In fact, scientific studies have proven the effects of the amygdala and attribute it to the cause of anger, resentment, depression, and many other emotional manifestations.

Assuming God is correct in His end-times analysis and that changes will continue to increase as even the heavens are shaken, it stands to reason that my lizard brain may be overwhelmed with natural fear and survival tactics. The more change that forces my lizard brain to kick in, the more fearful imaginations will arise and haunt me. Some of the imaginations will haunt me for only a few seconds, while others will haunt me for years. Collectively, and without faith, my human frailty and fearful imaginations will cause unpleasant side effects. The only way to offset this fear is to allow faith to flow and bring me to a higher level of operation, which will please God and allow me to be victorious.

God's Word helps us come to the conclusion that there will be only one way to live, and that one way is by faith! In the Old Testament and New Testament the shortest statement of how God's people are to live sure sounds like a mandate to me:

The just shall live by faith. (Habakkuk 2:4, Romans 1:17)

If you are on a sports team, in a family, working on critical projects, or leading a team of people, you will always have to balance and test in which direction everyone's fear and faith pendulum is swinging. If the sum of all the fear around the table is greater than all the faith around the table, the chances that your decision is pleasing to God is fairly slim. However, if the sum of the total faith is greater than the natural fears, you may find that God is well pleased and will act on your behalf. Even though this sounds simple and harsh, it is exactly the balance and outcome of Hebrews 11:6:

And without faith it is impossible to please God, because anyone who comes to him must believe that he exists and that he rewards those who earnestly seek him. (Hebrews 11:6)

Even though we recognize that human fear is driven by the lizard brain, when people use faith they balance the equation and put the outcome on God's side. Considering that God created the human brain, He knew that the amygdala controls our fears, anxieties, depression, anger, and all other emotions and stress. For this reason He evens out the playing field and uses the metaphor of a grain of mustard seed, 1/100 the size of an almond, to indicate we could move mountains with faith versus fear. Jesus states, "If you have faith as small as a mustard seed, you can say to this mountain, 'Move from here to there' and it will move. Nothing will be impossible for you" (Matthew 17:20). No wonder we are fearfully and wonderfully made. We can have fear, yet we can do wonders with the simple act of faith.

Seeing the Kingdom of Heaven While Exceeding the Righteousness of the Pharisees

Many people have been perplexed with the statement, "Unless your righteousness exceeds the righteousness of the Pharisees you cannot enter the Kingdom of Heaven" (Matthew 5:20). The reason Jesus was so serious about this is that the Pharisees spent their time fearing what Jesus was doing. They let their lizard brains control their fears and could not muster up enough faith to believe that Jesus was sent from God.

The Pharisees sat around the table discussing all the risks, concerns, fears, worries, and changes that would be required of them if they believed in Jesus. They realized that their form of religion would not survive the kind of changes Jesus was demonstrating. The miracles, signs, wonders, healings, and speaking with authority was a direct threat to their survival. Their lizard brains kicked into high gear, and they did exactly what Seth Godin predicted—they performed fight or flight. Their logic told them to fight as Jesus and his twelve disciples were few in number. Their choice to fight forced them to crucify the one who threatened their survival. They completely ignored their opportunity to utilize any faith and operated in their human fear. Their lack of faith showed they had no righteousness.

Considering that the only way to earn righteousness is through faith, the Pharisees had absolutely no righteousness. If they would have had even a grain of faith, they would have overruled their fear of losing their religious standing and embraced what Jesus represented. For this reason Jesus stayed focused on reminding us that we will not enter the kingdom of heaven without the kind of faith that produces righteousness. The good news is that the Pharisees had no faith and therefore no righteousness. The Pharisees may have been morally holy as well as prim and proper churchmen, but they operated in human fear to save their own religious bacon. In the end, their religious bacon sizzled and burned as Jesus tore the temple curtain in two! (Matthew 27:51).

> For in the gospel a righteousness from God is revealed, a righteousness that is by faith from first to last, just as it is written: "The righteous will live by faith." (Romans 1:17).

What this means for all of us who are willing, ready, and able is that even faith as small as a mustard seed will allow us to exceed the Pharisees' righteousness and enter the kingdom of heaven. I believe that each iteration and generation of heavenly understanding will bring us closer to appreciating, respecting, seeing, and entering heavenly realms. This kind of faith will allow the lower levels of religious survival to drop by the wayside and let us all soar in the heavenly realms of the kingdom. The only thing holding us back is the fear of our religious survival. You don't have to take my word for it, but please take Jesus's word for it. His promise can be found in Matthew 24:1–3, in which he foretells the ultimate decay of religion in order to bring one church without spot or wrinkle into His presence.

May we all appreciate the fact that we are fearfully and wonderfully made! It is completely normal to be fearful during the times that our lizard brains kick in. However, it is also necessary to reach out to God with faith during the times He asks us to rise up, stand up, speak up, and look up as His redemption continues to draw near!

Remember, few people or religions have tainted the image of heaven, so as we all approach a clearer and nearer vision of heaven, the more of common Christ-likeness we will find! With enough iterations of heavenly knowledge we will eventually become the one body that Christ has always desired and is ultimately preparing.

BIBLIOGRAPHY

Brill. (n.d.). The World Christian Database.

Dr. Jeffrey Long. (2012, May 02). *How Many NDEs Occur in the United States Every Day?* Retrieved May 2, 2012, from Near Death Experience Research Foundation: http://www.nderf.org/NDERF/Research/number_nde_usa.htm.

Journal, A. M. (2011). *You Must Be Dreaming: Creatively Solving Your Problems While You Sleep.* The American Mind Journal.

Koninklijke. (n.d.). World Religion Database. *International religious demographic statistics and sources.* (P. A. Edited by Todd M. Johnson, Ed.) Brill, NV.

LeClaire, J. (2012). *Dream, Visions Moving Muslims to Christ.* Lake Mary, FL: Charisma.

Lema, J. (2007). *Into the Light: Real Life Stories about Angelic Visits, Visions of the Afterlife, and Other Pre-Death Experiences.* New Page Books.

Malarkey, K. (2011). *The Boy Who Came Back from Heaven: A Remarkable Account of Miracles, Angels, and Life beyond This World.* Tyndale House Publishers.

Piper, D. (2004). *90 Minutes in Heaven: A True Story of Death and Life.* Revell.

Prothero, S. (2011). *God is Not One: The Eight Rival Religions That Run the World.* HarperOne.

Rico, D. (2011, December 08). *Scientists investigate water memory.* Retrieved May 12, 2012, from OdeWire: http://odewire.com/170441/scientists-investigate-water-memory.html.

Todd Burpo, L. V. (November). *Heaven Is For Real: A Little Boy's Astounding Story of His Trip to Heaven and Back.* Thomas Nelson.

Wescott Marketing. (2007, February). More than Dreams. Westcott. Retrieved from http://shop.cbn.com/product.asp?sku=5557869921

World, e. (2012, February). *Discover Your Mission.* Retrieved July 2, 2012, from e3 World Missions: http://www.e3partners.org.

ADDITIONAL BOOKS BY MICHAEL MATHEWS

And God Chose Dreams: To Elevate our Thoughts and Minds During Times of Change (ISBN-10: 1438933819, ISBN-13: 978-1438933818; can be purchased at AuthorHouse.com, Amazon.Com, and Barnes & Noble)

What in Heaven and Hell is Happening? A Modern Day Spiritual Timeline (ISBN-10: 143436125X, ISBN-13: 978-1434361257; can be purchased at AuthorHouse.com, Amazon.Com, Borders, and Barnes & Noble)

The Pearl Within: An Interactive and Personal Journey (Gospel Publishing House, Available from Focusonheaven.com)